Bower Farm
Riding Stables

Bower House Stables

St Thomas, Noak Hill

HAVERING VILLAGE
ARDLEIGH GREEN
and
THE HAROLDS

A Pictorial History

To Fred..

HAVERING VILLAGE
ARDLEIGH GREEN
and
THE HAROLDS

A Pictorial History

Chris Saltmarsh
and
Norma Jennings

PHILLIMORE

2009

Published by
PHILLIMORE & CO. LTD
Chichester, West Sussex, England
www.phillimore.co.uk
www.thehistorypress.co.uk

ISBN 978-1-86077-552-9

Printed and bound in Great Britain.

This book is dedicated to:

Chris's wife, Karen, and his sons,
Fionn, Archie and Jedd

and

the memory of Margaret and Frank Willcocks,
who both contributed so much to the life
of the London Borough of Havering.

If I were to own this countryside
As far as a man in a day could ride,
And the Tyes were mine for giving or letting,
Wingle Tye and Margaretting
Tye, and Skreens, Gooshays, and Cockerells,
Shellow, Rochetts, Bandish, and Pickerells,
Martins, Lambkins, and Lillyputs,
Their copses, ponds, roads, and ruts,
Fields where plough-horses steam and plovers
Fling and whimper, hedges that lovers
Love, and orchards, shrubberies, walls
Where the sun untroubled by north wind falls,
And single trees where the thrush sings well
His proverbs untranslatable,
I would give them all to my son
If he would let me any one
For a song, a blackbird's song, at dawn.

From 'If I were to own' by Edward Thomas

List of Illustrations

Frontispiece: Shepherds Hill, *c.*1930.

Acknowledgements

We should like to acknowledge, with gratitude, Roy Alexander for the superb line drawings he executed especially for the endpapers of our book. We should also like to thank those who have assisted us by contributing information or photographs, notably: the Amana Trust at Bower House; Patrick Baxter; Fay Chapman of the Essex Wildlife Trust at Bedfords Park; Mrs Clarke; Simon Donohue, Havering's local studies librarian; Jenny Engel; Essex Record Office, who permitted us to use illustration nos 4, 5a, 7, 21 and 41; Wenonah Faulkener; Arthur Flanders; James Green; Peter Haddon; Eddie Haley; Harold Wood hospital especially Angie Smith; Harold Wood Women's Institute; Harry Knightbridge; the Leach family of Harold Wood Coaches; Graham Martin; Edward Miller; Mr Morris, the Headmaster of Ardleigh Green Junior School; Redden Court Past Pupils' Association, particularly Mary Dodson, Vera Harrison and Courtney Kitching; Redden Court School; Andrew Skingley; Bernard Stevens; John 'Bunny' Warren, the Ardleigh Green historian; Peter Watt and Colin Welsch. Many of the photographs come from the personal collection of Chris Saltmarsh.

Despite our best efforts, we have been unable to trace the original ownership of a number of photographs and postcards, the latest dating back at least fifty years, which have proved invaluable to us.

Within Living Memory

In 1970, in a series of radio programmes edited by Lord Ritchie Calder, it was asserted that 'Man has changed the terms of his existence more in the past 25 years than in the previous 10,000 years. In the space of one generation—in the lifetime of the children born since 1945—we have telescoped eras each as significant as the Bronze Age, the Iron Age, the Renaissance, and the Industrial Revolution. We have mushroomed into the Atomic Age, been programmed into the Computer Age and been rocketed into the Space Age.' It can come as no surprise, therefore, that the recollections of the first of those children, now in their sixth decade, seem to be lodged in a more distant past than the 1950s and '60s: when the place of the working-class mother was firmly in the home without the benefit of central heating, unlimited supplies of hot water, refrigerators, freezers and washing machines. But, if bathrooms were either ice-cold in winter, or warmed with rather primitive oil heaters, it was remarkable that each home then possessed a bath and an indoor toilet. If shopping were a daily chore in a variety of small establishments to ensure food retained its freshness, at least the housewife wasn't an anonymous face in a supermarket queue.

Few such families could boast of a car, telephone or television, the last making an impact in 1953 in preparation for the coronation of our present Queen. One of the local Romford newspapers reported that in the very long North Hill Drive, on Harold Hill, the only two families possessing a television entertained, between them, 120 children on that day!

Only 19 years earlier, in 1934, at Ardleigh Green Primary School, wherein lodged the first wave of the Redden Court Secondary School pupils awaiting the erection of their new premises, flat irons were ranged upon the ironing stove in the Domestic Science room. Four years later, then in his own building, the headmaster of Redden Court was to record in his official log that the girls visited the electricity showrooms for a demonstration of all the new appliances. To this day, a gas lamp survives in both Ardleigh Green School and Harold Court School, which opened in 1929 as Church Road Council School. There would be no telephones at either establishment much before 1936, prior to which urgent messages had to be telegraphed.

An Earlier Chronicler

Progress had been exceptionally slow in the area since the prosperity anticipated by the opening of a railway station in 1868 had failed to materialise. Thus Harold Wood and its environs still possessed a rural feel when the young Maisie MacDonald came to live there sometime between the end of the First World War and the beginning of the construction of the Southend Arterial Road early in the 1920s. She recalled the sensation it caused when every morning and evening 500 men walked up from the railway station to the road-building site at the top of Squirrels Heath Road, known locally as Roper's Hill after the farmer at New Redden Court. Here, on the fringe of the village, lived the middle classes who were mortally offended by the uncouth, 'terrible' labourers.

Maisie and her family had travelled up from the increasingly urbanised surroundings of Manor Park to look for a house in the country. On arriving at Romford, the morning train for Harold Wood had already left and they were advised to take one to Squirrels Heath Station (now Gidea Park) and walk the mile from there.

> I can remember us all trudging along Squirrels Heath Lane, but how pretty it was—trees lining it on both sides and meeting over the top. We came to know it as the Shady Lane. I think there were two cottages only in the whole road, by a little stream, and then we turned into Ardleigh Green where there was the little baker's and a house with a peach tree growing up the side. On we went, passing half-a-dozen houses, Old Redden Court among them, and the farm of New Redden Court lying back on the right hand side. Following the directions, we turned at the little school into Gubbins Lane and saw the railway bridge before us.

Houses For Sale

Maisie recorded that her family rented one of the few houses in Gubbins Lane for 15s. a week, commenting that 'no-one seemed to buy houses then'. Homes were let out by the wealthy landowners of the time, generally to tenants who worked for them rather than with any intention of making large profits. By the end of her narrative, however, Maisie was aware of the changing times: 'My childhood was over and Harold Wood was beginning to change and expand—house building started, the population grew and eventually weddings could be held at St Peter's instead of the mother church at Hornchurch.'

Just as today, bricks and mortar were proving to be a most profitable investment. In the previous century developers may have burned their fingers when the railway station opened, but the area was ripe for change following the inevitable population migration from the increasingly congested London suburbs after the First World War and the opening of the Southend Arterial Road in 1925. By the 1930s, the farmlands surrounding the old village at Harold Wood had all been sold off for house building while the small hamlet of Ardleigh Green, which had been little affected by the construction of the Emerson Park Estate at its northern end in 1909, found itself at the centre of a housing boom.

In Havering-atte-Bower, where the population had always been sparse owing to the enormous amount of parkland surrounding the village, the process took longer and it was not until after the Second World War that the lands of Havering Park and Pyrgo Park fell into the hands of T.F. Nash Properties Ltd, who had been responsible for much of the house building in Collier Row. However, this time the developers were thwarted by the post-war metropolitan Green Belt legislation, which prevented further house building in the north of the borough. The hamlet of Noak Hill avoided development for the same reason, although not before the lands of Dagnams had been sold for the building of the Harold Hill Estate in the late 1940s.

Upminster Common escaped the grasp of the developers by a whisker. Essex County Council, as Lord of the Manor, was charged with upholding the rights of the residents but, following the requisition of the common for agricultural use on the outbreak of the Second World War, the county council reneged on its agreement to return it to the people. Only a strong campaign against the might of the politicians, launched by Edward Luther of Ardleigh Green and other local residents, preserved the common for public access. In Luther's own words, 'I already knew that common land was sacred to the people, but you had to be very quick to forestall those who regarded it as common game to be poached.'

The Nouveau Riche

The symbiotic relationship which had once existed between landlord and tenant was no more obvious than in the village of Havering-atte-Bower where almost everyone was employed by the owners of the grand houses, either in service or on the land of the estates' farms. Despite the accepted servitude of the lower classes, however, the rich landowners were not oblivious to the poor quality of life of their servants, upon whose devoted skills they depended, and proved generous benefactors over the centuries, helping, for example, to finance the school, village hall and church.

Winifred Popplewell, reminiscing about her childhood in the village at the turn of the 20th century, remembers the competition existing between the two major benefactors of the time, the Mcintosh and Pemberton-Barnes families, in their efforts to subsidise the church in particular. She provides a glimpse of that world of privilege, recalling that when the Lady of the Manor, Mrs McIntosh, passed by in her horse-drawn carriage the schoolchildren were expected to curtsey or bow. With the increased social awareness of the time, however, Winifred's mother said 'it wasn't necessary for her to do so as father was a tradesman'. Incidentally, Winifred describes how he, a tailor, sat cross-legged on a board in his shop window stitching the liveries for the servants of the élite.

By this time, most of the titled landowners of ancient prerogative had been replaced by the gentleman esquire, he of obscure origin who had gained prestige through the acquisition of money generated by the Industrial Revolution. When the royal lands of the whole Liberty of Havering-atte-Bower were disposed of in 1828, the manor of Havering village, together with Romford market, was bought by Hugh McIntosh, who had made his fortune as a contractor on the London docks, later supplementing his income with the advent of the railway. On his death, the manor passed to his nephew, David McIntosh, and eventually—by virtue of the Married Woman's Property Act of 1831—to David's widow.

Her humble title did nothing to curtail the pretensions of Mrs McIntosh, who anyway was descended from an aristocratic family on her mother's side. But money talked, whether in the hands of the nobility or the parvenu. Little wonder, then, that James Theobald Esq., Conservative MP for Romford in 1886, kept a larger retinue of servants in his residence of Bedfords than did Sir Thomas Neave, Baronet, in his country seat of Dagnams in neighbouring Noak Hill. An elaborate household and lifestyle became typical of professional families and the lesser gentry in an attempt to ape their 'betters'.

In Harold Wood, John Compton, a retired army tailor, had acquired the ancient manorial lands of Great Gubbins for a snip in 1876 from the bankrupted Harold Wood Estate Company. He thereafter built The Grange in 1884 and proceeded to set himself up as the local squire, providing employment in his brickworks and putting up money and land for the small school on the corner of Squirrels Heath Road and Gubbins Lane.

Other notable worthies were Edward Bryant, JP, of Bryant and May match fame, who donated his entertainment hall in Gubbins Lane for a war memorial, and Sir Joseph Broodbank, knighted in 1917 for his war work with the Port of London Authority, who took over as village squire in the style of John Compton and, later, W.G. Watson of the Tate and Lyle family. Maisie Macdonald recalls him living at Longmoor House:

> What tone this gave to Gubbins Lane! He always spoke to the children and, although we didn't exactly touch a forelock, we used to feel pleased. Lady Broodbank would have a day's shopping in London and the memory comes back to me of the station master accompanying her from the train carrying her parcels up Oak Road.

Ironically, when in the 1940s Longmoor House had become a reformatory school, 'a borstal', one of its earliest inmates, Eric Hebborn, in his autobiography *Confessions of a Master Forger*, described its appearance: 'It had once been a private dwelling, but one hesitates even to imagine its original occupants. No tree or shrub or flower mellowed its bricks or attended its curtainless windows.' In stark contrast to this future notorious art forger were the most renowned members of the new style of aristocracy, James and George Matthews. Beginning from humble premises in 1895 in Fitzilian Avenue, they were to head a corn chandlery and animal feed business which would spread throughout Essex. When St Peter's Church was built in 1938, purely by public subscription, it was the Matthews brothers, as the main benefactors, who were given the honour of laying the foundation stone.

At the other end of the spectrum, the Banyard family of Ardleigh Green, who could trace their lineage back to the Norman Conquest, had been reduced to dairy farming at Little Nelmes Farm from the latter part of the 19th century until the land was sold for housing in 1979. Nevertheless, they had not been slow to profit from the new prosperity generated by the population explosion between the wars, opening milk depots in both Hornchurch and Romford; nor were they able to resist the consequent building boom, involving themselves in housing development in Hornchurch and Gidea Park. By the 1930s the Banyard family had become one of the hamlet's main benefactors, as a result of which its coat of arms was later adopted as the badge of Ardleigh Green School.

Education For All

During the 19th century, the rapidly changing character of the country from agricultural to industrial was accompanied by a realisation that the new prosperity derived from it could not be maintained if the majority of the populace remained illiterate and uneducated. Prior to this, education had been the prerogative of the rich male. A son had to make his way in the world but the daughter of a well-to-do family was expected to marry and devote her life to children and domestic matters. It was still very much a man's world until the 1914-18 war.

In poor homes it was considered that children of either gender had little use of schoolroom learning for the physical exertions which would be expected of them in adult life. It was, therefore, a far-sighted philanthropist indeed, in the shape of Dame Anne Tipping, who endowed a school in Havering-atte-Bower as early as 1724 for the education of 20 poor girls and boys. This would be the foundation of the present village school, Dame Tipping Church of England School. More than a hundred years later, to meet the more pressing needs of the century, a church school opened in Noak Hill in 1848 while, in Harold Wood, a school was founded in 1886 on private subscription and government grant.

Further Expansion
In Havering village, Winifred Popplewell may have remembered the deference due to Mrs McIntosh in her position both as Lady of the Manor and benefactress of the school but, in Harold Wood, Maisie McDonald recalls jumping up and down with a friend outside the classroom window of an unpopular teacher chanting over and over, 'Old black rat'. Such rudeness, it would appear, is not just the prerogative of the early

21st-century child but more the result of a rapidly growing, diverse community. In a belated attempt to remove Maisie from the unwelcome influence of others, her mother sent her to Frome House private school at Miss Gladstone's in Athelstan Road.

To keep pace with the increasing population, the main school in Harold Wood had, by then, been adopted by the local authority and renamed Gubbins Lane Mixed Council School. In 1929 pressure was further eased by the opening of the Church Road Mixed Council School in Harold Park, a developing suburb of Harold Wood.

The growing pressure for provision of a secondary tier of education in Harold Wood resulted in both council schools being reorganised exclusively for children under the age of 11, while those over that age would be absorbed, from 1933, into the newly opened Ardleigh Green Council School, itself purpose-built for younger children. Intended as a more temporary measure than it would turn out to be, by 1935 the overcrowding was so severe that Mr Williams, who was already presiding there as headmaster of the embryonic Redden Court Senior School, decided to visit the site of the new school. He found only three builders, none of whom were working, and the contractor making no effort to complete it.

It would not be until the beginning of 1938, when a few classes in the permanent building were opened, that Mr Williams was able to hand some classrooms back to the headmaster of Ardleigh Green, Mr Barnes. In June of that year the Redden Court Senior Council School was officially opened in Harold Wood.

Later Problems

The sheer volume of people descending upon the L.C.C. housing estate at Harold Hill from 1948 would have repercussions throughout the borough. Not only would they change the face of Romford's politics but so desperate was the need to house those made homeless during the Blitz that, initially, there were insufficient schools to cater for their children. By 1951 the primary schools were in place—all 10 of them, including one Roman Catholic school—but even they were bursting at the seams and a new one, Brookside, would be opened in 1957. There were, however, no schools ready for those of secondary age, who were consequently farmed out to Redden Court School in Harold Wood and others in Brentwood. The behaviour of these young people, already unsettled by wartime deprivation and permissiveness, caused the redoubtable Miss Nunn, by then deputy headmistress at Redden Court, to debouch to Suttons School in Hornchurch for the duration of their stay, returning only in 1955 with the opening of the first two senior schools on the estate: Harrowfields and Quarles, two enormous secondary modern schools with separate buildings for boys and girls.

It would be a rather more peaceful passage for the staff of Quarles secondary modern who, in their turn, played host to two streams from the smaller Harold Hill Grammar School, which had originated in 1955 but would not open until 1958. In the same year, Broxhill secondary modern originated in temporary premises at

Harrowfields secondary and Bosworth primary schools. Its permanent premises opened in 1960.

Wartime

After the Second World War, the building of Harold Hill housing estate sent shock-waves reverberating through Harold Wood. Up until then its residents had enjoyed unfettered access to miles of open countryside on three sides. Now, they had a council estate on their doorstep, overcrowded with dispossessed city folk with whom they had little in common. The newcomers' children were all but ruining the reputation enjoyed by the local secondary school while the sons and daughters of the tightly knit communities of Harold Wood and Harold Park were drawn like a magnet to the more exciting elements on the opposite side of the Colchester Road. The only sphere in which residents of Harold Hill had the edge over their neighbours was their experience of the Blitz. As far as they were concerned, Harold Wood had 'had it easy' during the war.

In comparison with the devastation wreaked upon the East End of London there was much truth to this, although the area was not without personal tragedy. There was one fatality at Upminster Common, 17 at Harold Wood and Harold Park and eight at Ardleigh Green. The worst incident occurred in February 1945 when a V2 rocket destroyed five houses in David Drive, Harold Park, accounting for 14 deaths and 36 serious casualties.

Noak Hill suffered several rocket bombardments with two serious casualties and even the small village of Havering-atte-Bower was not without its drama: no civilian casualties but the church was damaged by air raids in 1940, and in 1944 the young Arthur Flanders witnessed a badly maimed German twin-engine bomber, a Junkers 88, hurtle past his home in Liberty cottages. Crash-landing in the grounds of Havering Grange, the only member of the crew to survive was tenderly extricated from the wreckage and, after the war, he would return to the village to thank his rescuers. However, the German pilot who parachuted down in Little Nelmes Farm, Ardleigh Green, received a less than enthusiastic welcome when he was held at the point of pitchforks until the relevant authorities arrived to apprehend him.

Tribute to a Young Hero

Perhaps the most poignant episode of the period occurred in Cecil Avenue, Ardleigh Green, when a parachute mine destroyed three houses, in the process killing five and wounding 55 on 15 November 1940. Peter Watt, in his book *Hitler versus Havering*, tells the story of a young scout, Ronald Eke, aged 13, who was the first casualty to be located. Pinned beneath piles of masonry he gave the impression that he only had 'a few scratches' and insisted that rescuers first locate his mother and father. A doctor who had arrived at the scene wrote that:

> Although his own injuries were very severe, and that he was suffering great pain there can be no doubt whatever, he managed to keep a firm hold on himself and gave valuable information not only about his own family but also about the occupants of neighbouring houses. His extraction took a long time in the darkness and rain, yet he never complained, and only occasionally was a cry wrung from him when some movement in the debris sent a sharp pain through his already suffering frame.

When finally extricated, he was rushed to hospital where he died during an operation to remove both his arms and legs. It was some grim consolation to those attending that he had died without knowing that both his beloved parents had been killed too. The doctor's testimonial ensured that Ronald's gallantry would not go unrecognised and he was awarded posthumously the highest honour the Scout movement can bestow, the Bronze Cross. Ronald was a pupil formerly of Ardleigh Green Primary School and later of Redden Court Senior School.

Conflict in the Skies

Sirens had been wailing in earnest throughout Harold Wood from 16 August as the struggle for air supremacy in the Battle of Britain shifted from over the sea to the land. The headmaster's log for Redden Court school records no respite from air-raid warnings for 62 days and nights. The children would struggle into school quite exhausted, only to have their school day continually disrupted as they were shuttled between classrooms and air-raid shelters.

School log, 16 September 1940

> Air-raid during the night lasted from 8.10 p.m. to 5.40 a.m. and bombs were dropped in the district cutting the road at Shepherd's Hill. Registers were closed at 10.00 a.m. There was an alarm from 10.30 a.m. until 10.50 a.m. There was another alarm from 10.58 a.m. to 11.45 a.m. There was another alarm from 12.20 noon to 12.55 seriously upsetting dinner arrangements. It was impossible to serve dinners until 1.30 p.m. causing afternoon school to be rather late. At 2.15 p.m. there was another alarm lasting until 6.10 p.m. at which time school was dismissed.

He was kept busy, too, along with the heads of other local schools, meting out severe punishment to juvenile collectors of incendiary bombs, several of which had not yet exploded!

It was a child of nine, Geoff Walton, a pupil at Harold Court Primary School, who would experience the full force of the reality of the exciting diversions in the sky when he witnessed a Hurricane crashing into a house on the corner of Woodstock Avenue, close to the Colchester Road.

Geoff stood rooted to the spot as the stricken pilot was lifted from the plane, 'very, very carefully' and gently laid on the grass feet away from him.

> I was only nine years old and never before or since have I seen a sight such as this. Here
> before me was this poor man fighting for his life. I assumed he had been attacked from
> ahead and below, for there were bullet holes in the aircraft and the pilot, himself,
> had been hit several times. His flying suit was soaked in blood and engine oil and, to
> add to his injuries, on impact he had smashed his face into the gunsight immediately
> in front of him. He was terribly shot up and fighting for every breath.

It was then that the young Geoff would have a harsh lesson in human nature. 'By
this time there were scores of people on the scene. Some of them were even stepping
round the pilot and trying to get small pieces of the aircraft to keep as souvenirs.'

The pilot, P.O. W.B. Pattullo, died in Oldchurch Hospital the next day. Sixty
years later, still haunted by his experience, Geoff, together with Norman Jennings,
told the story of their search for the pilot's family in their book, *The Search for
One of The Few.*

Harold Wood Hospital
The End of an Era

Both Ronald Eke and Pilot Officer Pattullo were taken to Oldchurch Hospital in
Romford, as the emergency hospital at Harold Wood would not be established until
1941 in the grounds of The Grange. After the war it continued initially as a geriatric
hospital but, by 1948, 12 acute and surgical wards were opened, one of which was
for children. This became the foundation of an important hospital which served a
vital role in the latter part of the 20th century for the Barking and Havering health
authority. In the opening years of the new millennium, however, both Harold Wood
and Oldchurch hospitals became casualties in the wake of a new flagship hospital:
Queen's in Romford.

For staff at Harold Wood Hospital, however, the end of an era had arrived some
thirty years before, in 1974, when the last matron left the hospital to make way
for a different style of administration. The role of the matron coloured everyone's
reminiscences, medical staff and patients alike.

Miss Lilian Chadd, secretary to the Matron, Miss Heasman, in 1948 recalled
that she was a very strict matron, especially with regard to the nurses' appearance
and manner. The Matron's office was in what had become the administrative centre
of the hospital, The Grange. Here, she would receive reports from her deputy and
assistant matrons, one of whom would be in charge of the nurses and wards and
the other of matters including catering and portering.

Mrs Margaret Connolly, speaking about her time as a cadet nurse in the 1960s,
reminds us that, even as late as this, there were very few married students and that
'if you wanted to marry you had to ask permission'. The Matron was very much
in charge and wards had to be immaculate with all the wheels on the beds facing

the same way. Ward rounds would be made during the day and night and just as important for the welfare of patients was the report given by the ward sister when a nurse changed ward: 'We would all queue outside Matron's office in The Grange at 9.00 a.m. on report day and we would be called in one by one.'

In 1970, Vince Maffei, who had just been appointed Senior Catering Manager, remembered the formality of the times. Matron Phillips, a formidable figure who would be the last to fulfil that role, 'visited the wards three times a day as well as the kitchens and dining rooms. There were two sittings for lunch and nobody could start eating until she arrived and gave the order to be seated.'

Those members of staff who had experience of life before and after Matron regret, as one, the disappearance of a 'hands-on' senior nursing figure and the rise of the managerial committee with all the attendant paperwork and computer power.

Village, Hill, Wood and Green

Charles I was the last king to survey the Royal Liberty of Havering-atte-Bower from the old palace of Edward the Confessor, across the royal hunting grounds of Harold's Wood to the town of Romford with its ancient market.

Today, no sign of the palace remains and the village of Havering-atte-Bower has lost the feudal air which existed well into the 20th century. But the shops at its heart are no more and most of its inhabitants work outside the village, conducting their leisure activities further afield. Despite being in a conservation area, it seems to have lost the old communal spirit. Strangers from outside the parish bounds patronise the newly extended village hall and successful school but a service is held in the church of St John the Evangelist every fortnight and, once a year, St Francis Hospice revives ancient customs on the green on May Day.

Ironically, the humble hamlet of Ardleigh Green, which sprouted up at a wide part of the old Green Lane leading through the forest of Essex to Hornchurch, has benefited from the modern-day development of which Havering village was deprived, for better or worse, owing to the post-war Green Belt legislation. Now fanning out on either side of the ribbon of road which was all it once comprised, Ardleigh Green has a thriving nucleus of shops, junior school and public house with a college of further education and two churches close by, giving it a quite separate identity from the mother parish of Hornchurch.

The woodland which stretched beyond Ardleigh Green, sweeping up to the heights of Havering-atte-Bower, has long been razed, its name poached by early developers as an identity for the proposed township of Harold Wood. Built on the ancient manorial lands of Great Gubbins and Redden Court in order to prosper from the coming of the railway, the present Harold Wood is neither town nor village but has settled into a comfortable existence as a dormitory suburb of

Romford. Nonetheless, together with Harold Park, it has retained much of its original independence, possessing churches, shopping parades, junior schools, a secondary school and many thriving recreational clubs and societies.

Of the old lands cloaked by forest, only Noak Hill has managed to retain its rural character despite standing on the fringe of the urban spread of Harold Hill, so called in the absence of the original name of Harold's Wood. Early attempts to name the estate Dagnams, after the manorial lands on which most of it stands, were defeated to avoid confusion with the town of Dagenham.

Built by the L.C.C. to accommodate many of those Londoners made homeless during the war, its reluctant landlord of Romford deemed, from the estate's inception, that it would not be permitted to develop into a long-term community owing to the large number of young people flooding the area. Once they had reached maturity and married they had to set up home elsewhere, while the industrial complex built to accommodate the new workforce in the late 1940s was wound up and the four secondary schools dwindled to one, of which, today, only half is occupied. Despite the area's revival in the 1980s following the sale of council homes to private owners, the surviving school—formerly Harrowfields and now King's Wood—would not be rejuvenated owing to a change in educational policy which allowed parents to breach the boundaries of their catchment area when choosing a school for their offspring.

Epitaph

Little remains of historical interest in the far north and north-east of Havering nor, for that matter, in any part of that vast borough; an indictment of the old towns of Romford and Hornchurch, which sought to capitalise on trade at the expense of history. But the ancient names live on in roads and public houses and in the poetry of Edward Thomas, who loved this small corner of the Essex countryside:

> What shall I give my daughter the younger
> More than will keep her from cold and hunger?
> I shall not give her anything.
> If she shared South Weald and Havering,
> Their acres, the two brooks running between,
> Paine's Brook and Weald Brook,
> With pewit, woodpecker, swan, and rook,
> She would be no richer than the queen
> Who once on a time sat in Havering Bower
> Alone, with the shadows, pleasure and power.

From *What Shall I Give?*

Havering-atte-Bower

1   The *Orange Tree* public house provided welcome respite for the cyclist, pedalling without the aid of gears, on the long climb up Orange Tree Hill to the village of Havering-atte-Bower standing 340 feet above sea level at the highest point of what is today the London Borough of Havering. The inn had been called the *Olive Tree* up until 1785.

2   In the village centre Elizabeth Row, pictured here at the beginning of the 20th century, faced the *Royal Oak* public house. The humble cottages were home to those who toiled in the fields or slaved in the large houses which had been built, since the demise of the royal palace, on the outskirts of the village.

3 Sadly derelict and awaiting demolition in 1967, Elizabeth Row would just escape rescue by an Act of Parliament passed the following year to ensure the preservation of our vernacular architecture.

4 The baker's boy strolls past the famous stocks and whipping post in this late Victorian engraving. The majestic elm, which had stood sentinel for centuries, was destroyed towards the end of the 1960s for reasons of safety.

5a and b   The 1877 Court Leet for Havering-atte-Bower recorded offences which resonate today: 'persons loitering at the corners of streets; children sliding upon the pavement; the chalking upon and defacing and injuring shop fronts, walls and fences'. Whether or not these warranted punishment in the stocks is not recorded but it is clear from this photograph that they had no serious purpose in Edwardian times, when this bespectacled gentleman perched upon them to survey the village green before smoking his pipe (left) or when this charming group was captured on camera (above).

6   By the middle of the 20th century it had become obvious that the old instruments of retribution had themselves to be protected from the attention of those who, in a past age, would have earned closer acquaintance with them. Today, a replica of the stocks and whipping post stands on the village green.

7   (Above left) It is now suspected that before the 16th century no church stood on the present site overlooking the village green, the Norman font originating from the first of the royal chapels annexed to Havering Palace. The architect's drawing of 1876 shows that a new church, paid for by public donation, would have a tower instead of a spirelet.

8   (Above) In the early years of the 20th century, when virtually all correspondence was via the written word or telegram, each post office, no matter how small, was a vital channel of communication. Here, in Havering, it stood adjacent the village green facing onto Orange Tree Hill.

9   (Left) The village green was at the heart of the community. Here, in the late 1950s, children stand on the edge of the green in preparation for Guy Fawkes' Night, the smithy behind them to the right and the local butcher's, Knightbridge, to the left. The family had been purveyors of meat since 1875. It would be the last shop to close over 100 years later.

10   (Above) Young Harry
Knightbridge, born 1949,
thoroughly deserves his place
in this prize-winning team
for his efforts in helping to
make sausages after school.
In a staged tableau, his uncle,
Frank Knightbridge, wields
the by then redundant poleaxe
while his father, John, grasps
the modern, humane, killing
instrument.

11   The role of the blacksmith
had become increasingly
superfluous by the time Con
Rowland was photographed
shoeing a horse from the
neighbouring riding school
in the 1960s. The elderly
gentleman in the photograph
was one of many passers-by
drawn to the smithy as if by a
magnet.

12 (Above) Maypole dancing on the green in the 1950s recalls the past vibrancy of Havering-atte-Bower. Today, St Francis hospice hosts the traditional May Fair when the now quiet village is revitalised.

13 Looking down North Road in 1920, from the direction of the green, the *Royal Oak* can be seen on the left opposite Elizabeth Row. The timber-framed, weatherboarded house in the foreground, Rose Cottage, was built in the 17th century.

NOTED FOR

Mason
and FAMILY

HAVERING-ATTE-BOWER

Provisions . Grocery . Hardware

Phone: HAVERING 1

HOME
COOKED
HAM

POST . . . . TELEGRAPH
and MONEY ORDER OFFICE

14 (Above) Three decades later, the scene has retained its sleepy aspect but it can be seen that the road is now clearly separated from the footpaths by kerbs while the view is dominated by a telegraph pole. With a large shopping centre barely a mile away in Collier Row, and the consequent closure of most of the old family businesses, Rose Cottage became a post office and general store to cater for the villagers' basic needs.

15 The Mason family had run Rose Cottage as a grocery store since 1924. Their 1950s business card indicates that it was also in competition with Knightbridge, the butcher.

16 The first school, endowed by Dame Anne Tipping in 1724 for the education of 20 children, was situated close to the village green but, after a chequered history, it was rebuilt in North Road in 1837 to accommodate 60 pupils and again for 126 in 1891. The school is pictured here on Thursday 20 May 1858 when its pupils were being marshalled in preparation for a special church service on behalf of day and Sunday schools.

17   Sent in 1928, this postcard presents a view of North Road looking towards the school in the distance.

18   The sons of the ruling classes are singled out by virtue of their starched collars and sailor suits. The poorer boys would leave the small village school to work on the land or in factories while the girls would be expected to marry or go into service. This photograph, however, was taken four years before the First World War and the beginning of the breakdown of the old social order, after which nothing would ever be the same.

19 (Above) Beyond the school, on the outer regions of the village, this row of 1920s council houses (pictured a decade later) would mark the limit of building in Havering-atte-Bower following the imposition of the metropolitan Green Belt after the Second World War. They were named Liberty Cottages following a competition held at the school.

20 At the other end of the spectrum, on Orange Tree Hill, Bower House is one of only two Grade I listed domestic buildings in the vast London Borough of Havering. Built in 1729 and pictured here in a 19th-century engraving, its importance lies in an inscription in the entrance hall, 'From the remains of the royal palace of Havering Bower, situated on the summit of the hill, this dwelling was founded.'

21 Close by, sandwiched between Lower Bedfords Road and Broxhill Road, Bedfords House was not so fortunate despite its more legitimate claim as a genuine manor house. Pictured here in 1819, surrounded by its beautiful grounds, it was sold to Romford in 1933 for use as a museum before being requisitioned during wartime for the National Fire Service. The mansion was demolished in 1959.

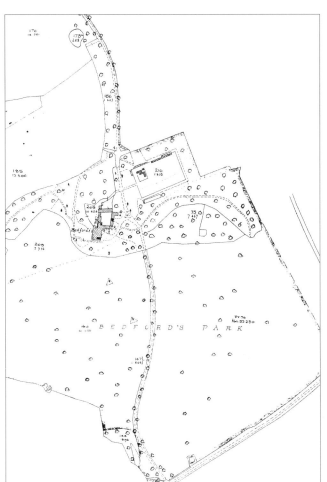

22 The site of Bedfords House is now occupied by a visitors' centre serving Bedfords Park, now approached from the tradesman's drive at the top of the map leading from Broxhill Road. The main drive was accessed from Lower Bedford Road at the bottom. Plans are afoot to restore the large, rectangular, walled garden in the top right-hand corner of the estate, against which stood the gardener's cottage, seen here as a small shaded area to the left of the path leading to the garden entrance.

23 By the turn of the 20th century, the L-shaped part of the house looking over the parkland had been squared off by the addition of a conservatory while an enormous bay window dominated the entrance. Now only the steps remain, leading down from the café in the new visitors' centre.

24 A vast number of servants was needed to maintain the lifestyle of the rich with teams employed in the house, the stables—in later years, the garages—and the gardens and parklands. James Reynolds, pictured with his family in 1918, was employed as a gardener at Bedfords for many years. His daughter, Alice May, standing behind him, would later marry one of the estate's groundsmen, John Haley.

25 In the early years of their married life, John and Alice lived in Gardener's Cottage at Bedfords together with their four eldest children: Alf—standing tall at the back of the photograph next to Joe—and John and Eddie perched on the arms of the sofa. What a wonderful playground they would have had! When their father took up a post as groundsman for Romford's parks in 1935, the family moved to Rush Green, where they were photographed in the 1950s.

26   No longer able to recruit the battery of servants needed to sustain it after the First World War, and lacking the finances to maintain it following the Second, the fate of Bedfords was sealed. But, at least, its parkland remains to this day as a lung for the residents of the increasingly congested town of Romford. The 1960s postcard features a picnic with ubiquitous Thermos flask, the deer enclosure and a view which, on a clear day, stretches across the River Thames to Kent.

27   On its way to what is now Harold Hill, Broxhill Road has passed, in the distance, the South Lodge of Pyrgo Park where the queens of England had their dower house, Pyrgo Palace. On the right of the road once lay brick fields, exhausted since before the end of the 19th century.

Harold Hill and Noak Hill

28 Broxhill Secondary Modern School lies at the Noak Hill Road junction where the grounds of Harold Hill Grammar have just nudged into the picture. In the late 1970s the two merged to form Bedfords Comprehensive School which was closed some twenty years later; a casualty of Romford's decision, at the outset, to curb Harold Hill's development as a long-term community.

29 The success of the secondary grammar school meant that these children of working-class origins at the fledgling Harold Hill Grammar School could aspire to a university education and career. Jacqueline Phillippe, seated fourth from the right on the front row, while training to become a teacher, met and married Julian 'Mo' Anthoine, one of the foremost mountaineers of his generation. Jackie, herself, became a climber of no mean note.

30　The modern-looking bicycle leaning against the wall of the *Bear* in the early years of the 20th century serves as a rude reminder that the predominant rural feel of a centuries-old way of life was under threat.

31　Pictured here in 1910, when known as the Romford Road, Noak Hill Road, today, has still managed to cling on to some of its rural character despite its proximity to Harold Hill. The thatched and weatherboarded cottage still survives as a Grade II listed building, its boarded façade now stripped away to reveal the timber frame beneath.

32　Directly after its junction with Church Road, Noak Hill Road becomes Chequers Road, called after the hostelry at its northern end which then lay in the parish of South Weald. The peaceful vista has since been violated by the London Orbital motorway, the M25, which now cuts a swathe through Noak Hill and the metropolitan Green Belt.

33 The pony has been stopped in its tracks to enable the photographer to capture this enchanting late Victorian scene in the Noak Hill countryside at Wright's Bridge, a small, sturdy wooden construction over the Putnam brook. The pretty hamlet of Noak Hill was a popular refuge from the noise and pollution of Romford town.

View from White's Bridge, Noak Hill Essex

*Dear Cissie,
This is
a little brook
which you can
see is running
very fast, which
proves that Essex
is not such a
flat county as
some people
suppose.
Your affect. Pa
J Wheatley*

34 Owing to the reconfiguration of roads caused by the construction of the motorway, the same view can only be obtained from what is now a narrow metal accommodation bridge lying in its shadow. The Putnam, or Weald, Brook runs as fast today as it did then when viewed from Wright's (not White's) Bridge, part of its course now culverted beneath the M25. The postcard is one of the earliest, the reverse side being used exclusively for the address.

35 The view along Church Road in 1910 is little changed today although the community, unlike Havering-atte-Bower, is no longer able to sustain the school pictured on the left. The building of St Thomas's Church was financed by the friends and family of the late Lady Neave, wife of Sir Thomas Neave, Bt, to fulfil her wish to have a church for the poorer residents of the hamlet who, until then, would have had to walk to the mother church in Romford.

36 This painting of the church was executed to celebrate its consecration on 29 April 1842. The young Elizabeth Fry, who attended the ceremony with her mother, recorded in her diary that the church was 'very pretty, though externally peculiarly plain'.

37 By the mid-1930s, Noak Hill was attracting enough day visitors from Romford to cause the Hammer family, of Pentowan Farm, to expand their general stores into a tearoom. Situated beyond the church, it was renamed the Pentowan Café and, although closing shortly after the war, it would remain on the destination boards of some of the 238 buses to Noak Hill for several years to come.

38 Dagnam Park, Noak Hill, was the seat of the Neave family until the Second World War, during which time it was occupied by the army. In the late 1940s the house, park and surrounding acreage—including the ancient manorial lands of Cockerells and Gooshayes—were sold to the L.C.C. for the building of Harold Hill housing estate. This O.S. map of 1895 shows the area to be occupied by its north-eastern section. The park itself would be retained as recreational space, while the house would be demolished. The original medieval building is marked on the map as 'Dagenhams—Remains of'.

39   The early house was remodelled in the 1660s when it was described by Samuel Pepys, who visited it in order to escape the plague in London, as being 'a most noble and pretty house that ever, for the bigness, I saw'. This engraving is dated 1769, after it had been extended.

40   A less flattering view shows how the addition of two wings has detracted from the pleasing proportions of the central house which Pepys had so admired. In 1772 it was rebuilt as a plain, brick, three-storey house typical of the late Georgian style.

41 The classical portico framing the front door, in imitation of the earlier building, relieves the spartan façade of the later house of Dagnams but, deserted and prey to vandals, the mood is sombre as the old house awaits demolition in the 1950s.

42 Such was the importance and wealth of the Neave family that, coupled with the needs of a still very rural labour force, they were able to maintain a full complement of servants following the First World War. Counted among the lower echelons of the servant hierarchy were the third housemaid, Mary, and John Elvin, the hall boy, who was 18 years old when photographed *c*.1930.

43 Because the moat surrounding the medieval manor house of Cockerells prohibited its expansion, another house was built on a site now occupied by Dycorts School, close to which the moat survives as a Scheduled Ancient Monument. Following the decay of the manorial system, the manor of Cockerells was absorbed into the Dagnam estate to become, eventually, Dagnam Park Farm, its ancient house pictured here *c*.1900 with Mr Walter Brooks, the tenant farmer, and his family.

44 On the opposite side of Dagnam Park, close to the Noak Hill Road, stood The Priory, which had been built as a dower house for the widows of Dagnam baronets when the estate descended to the first-born son. The house was demolished following bomb damage during the Second World War.

45 This section from an O.S. map of the late 1950s, replicating part of the extract from the earlier map of 1895, shows development in the area of Hatter's Wood on the right. In stark contrast to the urban spread, the rectangular moat of Cockerells is marked at the lower right-hand corner of the wood. Carters Brook runs through Central Park, above Gooshays roundabout, eventually becoming Paines brook, a tributary of the River Ingrebourne. Gooshays House itself was retained as a community centre until it was burned down.

46 The school featured right of centre on the previous map is Quarles Secondary Modern School, which opened in Tring Gardens in 1955, the girls' building easily identifiable by the netball courts. Named after a minor Essex poet of the 17th century, it later adopted the Neave family name when transformed into a comprehensive school.

47 Hilldene Farm, as advertised on this dairy cart in 1910, lent its name to one of the main arteries serving the estate, a primary school and the large central shopping area.

48 Farnham Road cuts through the middle of the Hilldene shops, a far cry from the previous rural idyll.

49 The access road in the foreground, running parallel to Hilldene Avenue, leads into Farnham Road and the Hilldene shopping centre, a large, utilitarian complex typical of the 1950s which serves as the estate's main shopping area, close to Central Park. Its very first business—a television shop—was opened by the comedic team of Jimmy Jewel and Ben Warris. It has changed so little today that only by scrutinising the models of cars can we ascertain that this photograph was taken in the 1960s.

50 The swimming bath that until recently dominated Central Park has been relegated to the history books to make way for an enormous new leisure centre, the progeny of a government-funded regeneration programme for the area.

51 The paddling pool in Central Park, pictured here in its early days, has long since gone; a reflection, perhaps, of the estate's dwindling child population.

52 Considering how the estate's reputation had suffered so much in its early days from the influx of an enormous number of young East Enders keen to establish a territory, it is warming to pay tribute to David Lamb, who in 1959 became the first Scout on Harold Hill to receive the Queen's Scout Badge.

53 A glimpse into the industrial part of the estate, which would employ most of the new residents of Harold Hill, captures the ladies of the Lovable Brassiere Company.

54 Situated on Hilldene Avenue, Bosworth Primary School, with its two storeys, was the largest on the estate. Small wonder, then, that it could take its pick of pupils for the football team, probably accounting for the number of reserves pictured here. The school was closed in 1974 owing to fears of collapse through the use of high alumina cement in its construction.

55 This rather pristine view of Amersham Road and Mead School c.1960, dominated by the mature oak which was a relic of the old manorial lands of Gooshayes, would today be littered with parked cars for, when the council estate was conceived, it could not be foreseen that people living in subsidised housing would ever be in a position to garage a car. Since the 1980s, an increasing change to private ownership has vastly exacerbated the problem throughout the whole area.

56 When opening the 1954 summer fête of the Church of the Most Holy Redeemer, Petersfield Avenue, the editor of the *Catholic Herald* pointed out that, in relation to the population of the parish, there was a higher proportion of Roman Catholics living in Harold Hill than anywhere else in the country. This eventually necessitated the building of a much bigger church, which the older one, pictured here, now serves as a hall.

57 In an earlier, unenlightened time, old houses had to earn their keep if they were not to be demolished to make way for housing development. New Hall, which had been constructed on the site of a much older house at the beginning of the 18th century, consequently became the *Morris Dancer* public house in Melksham Close. It is now protected as a Grade II Listed Building.

58 Today, Harold Hill is separated from the middle-class garden suburb of Gidea Park by the roundabout at Gallows Corner, the density of traffic which converges there obliterating all memory of the horse trotting meetings held in the vicinity up until the late 1950s. Ironically, 'trotting' has once more become popular along the rural lanes of Noak Hill, sometimes to the alarm of the unsuspecting motorist.

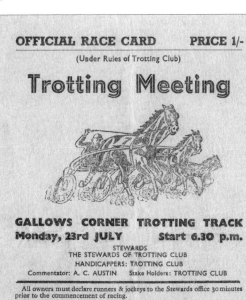

OFFICIAL RACE CARD   PRICE 1/-

(Under Rules of Trotting Club)

Trotting Meeting

GALLOWS CORNER TROTTING TRACK
Monday, 23rd JULY   Start 6.30 p.m.

STEWARDS
THE STEWARDS OF TROTTING CLUB
HANDICAPPERS: TROTTING CLUB
Commentator: A. C. AUSTIN   Stake Holders: TROTTING CLUB

All owners must declare runners & jockeys to the Stewards office 30 minutes prior to the commencement of racing.

If less than five runners in any race prize money will be reduced.

Saliva tests will be taken at the discretion of the Steward. When such a test is made all stake monies will be with-held until the result of the test is made known.

Only drivers taking part in the race will be allowed on the track.

A horse may be led to the start only by permission of the Stewards.

No horse can win if passing the winning post by any other 'gait' than a 'trot.'

Any horse that gains an advantage by breaking for any distance will be disqualified.

Any horse coming under starters orders will be considered a runner.

No person will be allowed to withdraw a horse that has once been on the track except by special permission of the Stewards.

Bookmakers are warned not to pay out until winning and second jockeys have been declared 'weighed in.'

In the event of an objection a red flag will be hoisted. A white flag will be hoisted if the objection is sustained. A blue flag will be hoisted if the objection is over-ruled.

★ *Whilst every precaution will be taken the organisers cannot be responsible for* ★
any accident whatsoever and reserve the right to refuse admission.

59   The profitable traffic generated at this meeting of the ways in the early 1900s caused the Old Hornchurch brewery to replace a humble tap room, known as the *Woodman*, with the *Plough*, behind which was situated a tearoom. In 1925, the brewery was bought by Mann, Crossman and Paulin, who enlarged the hostelry to coincide with the completion of the Southend Arterial Road. The *Plough* was closed in 2007.

60   It is hardly credible that, as late as the 1930s, Gallows Corner could ever have looked so peaceful and that a member of the public could stand there in such a casual fashion.

61   Perhaps a little more recognisable as the notorious Gallows Corner roundabout that we are familiar with today, this view in 1965 would be changed six years later when a temporary flyover was erected to ease increasing traffic congestion. It is still in place!

Harold Wood

62 By 1915, about the time when Maisie McDonald's family moved into Harold Wood, a small community had developed around the Great Eastern railway station. It boasted a few shops, a small 'tin' church and, lined with impressive poplar trees, Avenue Road, which had originally been part of a long drive stretching from the Roman road, now the A12, to The Grange, occupied by John Compton, the village's self-styled squire.

63 Maisie's description, in the introduction, of approaching Harold Wood resonates in this early photograph, the farmlands of New Redden Court lying on the right-hand side of Squirrels Heath Road and, just ahead on the left, the turning into Gubbins Lane, past the little school.

64 Gubbins Lane, which is now central to Harold Wood, was then on the fringe of the village. Here, in the early 1920s, looking down towards the A12 London to Colchester Road, only a few houses had been built close to the crossroads there. The houses beyond the fields line Arundel Road.

65 (Right) The Chapman and André map of 1777 shows the farmhouses of Little and Great Gubbins in relation to Dagnam Park, the future nuclei of Harold Wood and Harold Hill respectively, separated by the Roman road, which was then called the Great Essex Road.

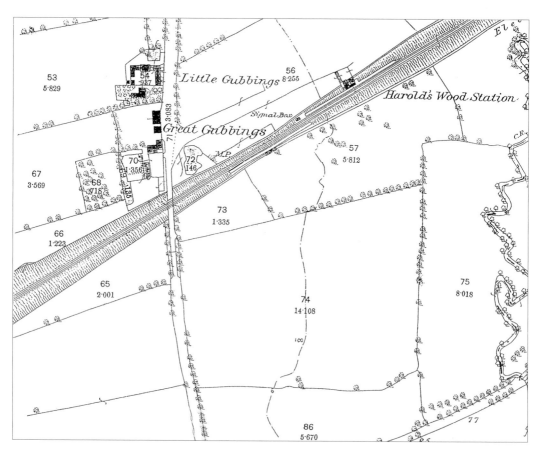

66 The survey of the area in 1866, indicating the path of the railway line, reveals just how rural it was. Apart from farms, there was no settlement in what would become known as Harold Wood, and labourers and servants would have lived at Ardleigh Green or Upminster Common. Also illustrated is the early abortive site of the booking hall, on the north side of the line, which prompted the building of the *King Harold*.

Navestock Side

Vicarage

Navestock Heath

Savage Green

Bentley Mill

Warren House

Moat

Bookham

Horseman Side

Ditchleys

Godfreys

Cox Green

Serpents Hall

Water Hale

Mill Hill

Weald Side

Jn.º Wright Esq

Great House

Dycoats

Doctors

Lang

..ons Green

Goose Wood

The Crooked Billet

Havering Plain

Wright's B.

Hoes

How Hatch Cap.t Smith

Wace hill Common

Howhatch Farm

S.r Jn.º Parker

The Lodge

Weald Hall

..e Towers Esq

Wooles

Nook Hill

Rich.d Neave Esq

SouthWeald

The Parsonage

Pains

Dagnam Park

Mayland

Brick Kiln

Cockerils

Weshy Bough

16 M

Brook Street

Moscalle

Gooses

Puttells Bridge

Puttells Lane

Hunger Down Farm

15 M

Dial House

Nags Head

Bowells

..mford ..mmon

New Hall

Tylers Hall

Jn.º Rudman Esq

Warley Place

Cap.t Adam

14 M

Gubbings

Tyler's Common

Warley

Brick Kiln

Street

..nam Hare Hall

..illing Esq

Brakes Place

Readen Court

Dagnam Common

Brick House

Realtetills

Edw.d James Esq

Owlets Hall

The Great House

L. Burdens

G. Burdens

Emery Farm

South House

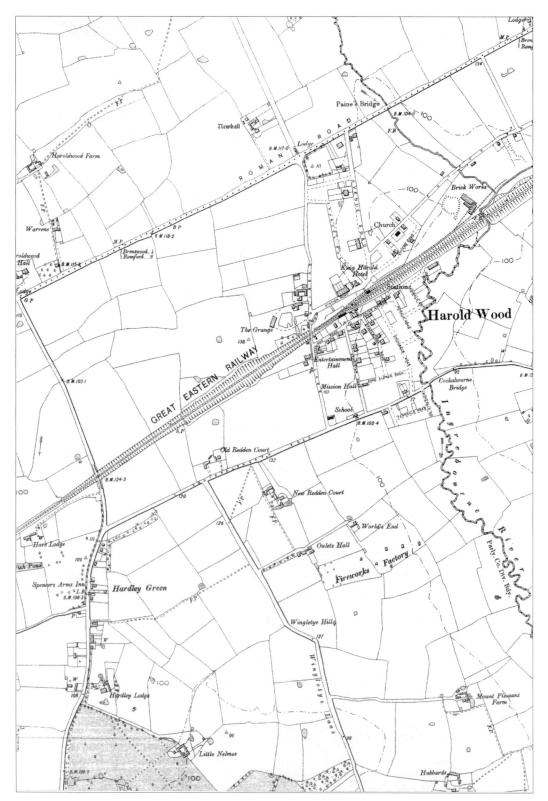

67 In this map of 1898 the intended site of the railway booking hall, close to the *King Harold*, provides access only to the platforms from the north of the line. On the opposite side, houses and shops cluster around the relocated main entrance, at the top of Athelstan Road, while Station Road would languish until the 1930s when the booking hall would be moved once again.

68 When the farm of Great Gubbins was sold shortly after the opening of the railway station in 1868, its proximity was seen purely as an advantage for transporting animals to market, the potential for more profitable investment not then having been envisaged.

LOT FOUR.

A VERY DESIRABLE FREEHOLD ESTATE,

KNOWN AS

GREAT GUBBING'S, OTHERWISE GREAT GOBINE'S FARM,

In the Parish of HORNCHURCH,

Situate abutting upon the South Side of the London Road, midway between the Market Town of Romford and Brentwood, and only 15 miles from London;

IT COMPRISES A

COMFORTABLE FARM HOUSE,

CONTAINING

Parlor, Keeping Room, Kitchen with Oven, Brewhouse, Dairy, and Beer Cellar, four Bed Rooms and Lumber Room,

WITH

GOOD GARDEN AND LARGE ORCHARD.

THE PREMISES COMPRISE

Poultry House, Two Barns with Oak Plank Floors, and Three lean-to Sheds, Piggeries, Stable for Five Cart Horses, Chaff-bin and Harness House, Cow House for Nine Cows, and Calf-Pens with Loft over, Wagon and Implement Sheds.

The whole of the Land lies in a Ring Fence, adjoining the premises; it is exceedingly well roaded. From its proximity to one of the best Corn and Cattle Markets in the County, and easy access by Railway, together with the fact of its being sound and productive Corn Land, with a fair proportion of superior Pasture, renders it certain at all times to command a good tenant.

THE WHOLE COMPRISES AN AREA OF

168 a.   3 r.   14 p.

AS SHEWN IN THE FOLLOWING SCHEDULE:

No. on Plan and Tithe Map.	Description	Cultivation	Quantities	No. on Plan and Tithe Map.	Description	Cultivation	Quantities
			a. r. p.		Brought forward...		a. r. p. 77 2 29
1229	Chalk Mead	Pasture	8 1 23	1257	Long Fourteen Acres	Arable	14 1 7
1229a	Slip	"	0 0 27	1258	Peyto's Bridge Mead	Pasture	4 3 13
1230	Seven Acres	"	7 3 2	1259	Ditto	"	4 3 4
1230a	Slip	"	0 0 24	1260	Highway Field	Arable	12 1 3
1230b	Willow Bed	Withies	0 1 32	1261	Middle Ten Acres	"	10 1 23
1231	Gravel Pit Field	Arable	8 1 14	1262	Stack Yard Field...	"	10 2 23
1232	Cow House Field	"	6 2 6	1263	Long Bone Field	"	8 1 6
1233	Part of ditto	Pasture	1 0 20	1263A	Rough and Pond	"	0 1 4
1234	Gravel Pit Field	"	5 1 24	1264	Little Ambers	"	7 0 13
1235	... ...	"	4 3 4	1265	Great Ambers	"	9 2 13
1236	Bone Field	Arable	9 2 0	1271	Little Coney Burrows	Pasture	3 2 37
1236a	Plantation	Wood	0 3 12	1271A	Homestead	"	2 0 28
1237	Torks Field	Arable	12 3 7	1272	Part of Great Coney Burrows	"	1 0 38
1256	Fourteen Acres	"	14 1 35	1272A	Lower ditto	Arable	1 2 16
	Carried forward ...		77 2 29		Total		168 3 14

This Estate is Freehold of ancient Demesne held of the Manor of Havering, subject to Quit-rents amounting to 17s. 4d. per annum. It was occupied for many years by the proprietor (the late RICHARD REYNOLDS, Esq.) until the time of his decease. Possession will be given upon completion of the purchase.

Land Tax £9 4s. per Annum.

NOTE.—The triangular piece of Land opposite the Farm Premises, as denoted on the Plan, is conveyed to the Eastern Counties Railway Company, under a special covenant as to the use thereof.

[5

69 Most of the houses close to the station entrance, like this one in Ronald Road photographed in 1910, were built for the working classes, the majority of whom were employed by the Great Eastern Railway Company. Some of the roads remain unfinished to this day.

70 The imposing *King Harold* might have missed out on the opportunity to profit from the passing trade brought by the railway but, as the only public house in the village centre, it was hardly likely to become impoverished.

71 With the station failing to fulfil its promise it became little more than a halt known as Paraffin Junction, owing to the lights ranged along a generally deserted platform. The original booking office, photographed here *c.*1918, seems to reflect that earlier desolation.

72 Turning our back on the railway station, we are presented with a wintry scene in Athelstan Road in 1908. Here, large villas for the anticipated influx of the middle classes had been built by the Harold Wood Estate Company in the 1860s to coincide with the opening of the railway station. The company's success was heavily dependent upon the creation of a township and when this did not materialise it was declared bankrupt.

73 As winter turns to spring, we are privileged to meet a memorable village schoolmaster, Thomas Rose, relaxing with his wife in their garden in Athelstan Road, *c*.1905. Both a great Shakespearean scholar and, well into his sixties, a notable badminton player, he lost his sight at the age of 80 after a failed cataract operation, whereupon he promptly taught himself Braille.

74 Thomas Rose lived at 'Sunnyside', the last house in this photograph on the corner of Athelstan Road and King Alfred Road, pictured here *c*.1915.

75 (Above left) The United Methodist Church, which originated in Athelstan Road in 1889, was replaced in 1929 by a new church on the corner of The Drive and Gubbins Lane, after which the redundant building was put to use as a commercial carpentry workshop.

76 (Left) By the beginning of the 20th century the railway station staff, under the leadership of Frederick Flegg, had expanded to cope with increased traffic. Mr Frank Miller, seated on the far left of the photograph, recalled that, in those times, a stationmaster enjoyed power, prestige and respect, not only among his employees but also in the wider community.

77 (Above right) In 1914, a group of naïve young soldiers pose happily for the photographer while awaiting the London train. It is left to us to wonder how many of them are commemorated on the Roll of Honour at the Harold Wood Memorial Hall.

78 (Right) It can be confirmed that W.A. Martin was one of the soldiers in the group who did not return home.

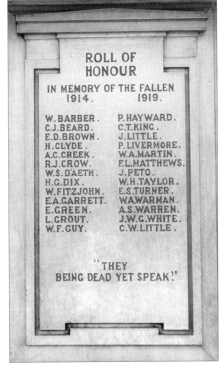

ROLL OF HONOUR

IN MEMORY OF THE FALLEN
1914.   1919.

W. BARBER .	P. HAYWARD .
C.J.BEARD .	C.T.KING .
E.D.BROWN .	J. LITTLE .
H.CLYDE .	P. LIVERMORE .
A.C.CREEK .	W.A.MARTIN .
R.J.CROW .	F.L.MATTHEWS .
W.S. D'AETH .	J. PETO .
H.G.DIX .	W.H.TAYLOR .
W.FITZJOHN .	E.S.TURNER .
E.A.GARRETT .	W.A.WARMAN .
E.GREEN .	A.S.WARREN .
L.CROUT .	J.W.G.WHITE .
W.F.GUY .	C.W.LITTLE .

"THEY
BEING DEAD YET SPEAK!"

79 Oak Road shops, pictured here *c.*1928, benefited from their position close to the railway booking hall until it was relocated during the following decade. A Pratt's spirit tanker can be seen on the left delivering fuel.

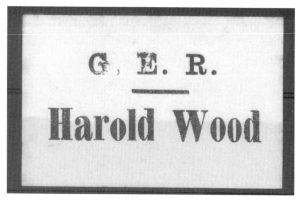

80 On the other side of the first booking hall, in 1915, the Fitzilian Avenue shops were also at the hub of the village although, again, this was all to change with the opening of a new station entrance in Gubbins Lane.

81 A Great Eastern Railway parcel label, *c.*1910.

82 An N7 Tank locomotive, running bunker first, leaves Harold Wood on its way to Liverpool Street Station during the 1920s. A stalwart of the suburban services, it was valued for its ability to accelerate over the comparatively short distances between stations.

83 This later view, taken from the same vantage point, shows the planning stages of the Gidea Park to Shenfield track-widening in the early 1930s, under the auspices of the London and North Eastern Railway Company. The goods yard to the left of the picture would be swallowed up during the process but a siding was maintained for coal deliveries on Station Road until at least 1965.

HAROLD WOOD

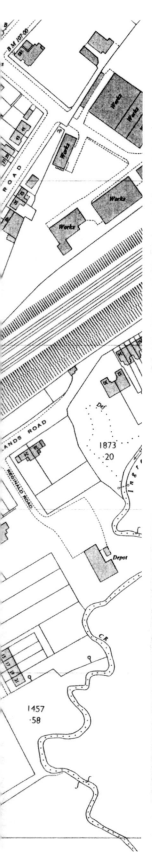

84 By 1945 the expanded railway line had brought that long sought after prosperity to Harold Wood. The old centre of the village is now virtually indistinguishable from the more recent development along Station Road but the first booking hall, and part of the curved drive leading to it, is visible at the top of Athelstan Road where it can be seen to this day.

85 The station entrance of the L.N.E.R. in 1965 was, in contrast to that of the G.E.R., raised high above the railway line.

86 The goods yard of that time, positioned behind the booking hall parallel with Station Road, is now used as a carpark but one of the old coal offices remains today as an estate agent's.

87 Station Road leads down from its junction with Gubbins Lane to Harold Park, *c*.1938, passing between its parade of shops on the left and the railway and goods yard on the right.

88 Photographed in 1965 at the top of Oak Road, on the opposite side of Gubbins Lane, Matthews' mill was once the cornerstone of an animal feed and seed distribution empire which spread throughout Essex. Sold to Unilever in 1963, it would be demolished five years later to make way for Holdbrook Close, named after the chief foreman who worked there.

89 Looking down Gubbins Lane from the mill towards the A12 in the 1950s, it would appear that Harold Wood has settled comfortably into its new role as a dormitory suburb of Romford, the shockwaves of its adolescence now some thirty years in the past.

90 The camera of the late 1920s, peering in the same direction, has captured the grim reality of the brutal transformation from country lane to suburban road, the march of the identical, featureless houses at odds with the grass footpath and dusty road.

91 (Clockwise from above left) These houses, too, present an incongruous sight, lining up, as it would seem, on either side of a stretch of meadow which would become Arundel Road *c*.1925.

92 Over a decade later, a transformed, well-established Arundel Road proves that the symmetry of man-made features can be quite pleasing to the eye.

93 The neatly planted entrance to The Ridgeway *c*.1938, with the impressive mock-Tudor houses so beloved of the 1920s and '30s, reflects an ideal image of suburban life, close to the countryside, which would eventually attract many to Harold Wood.

94 The top end of The Ridgeway tells another story, roughly carved from a field with its houses stranded in the distance. The residents, however, obviously relished their easy access to open space and are pictured here in the 1930s enjoying a picnic without the benefit of a barbecue or blaring stereo although, to the 21st-century eye, they appear to be dressed very formally for the occasion.

95 At the beginning of the 20th century, the hope of a property boom had long since fizzled out and The Grange was sold to the West Ham County Borough Council for use as a convalescent home. During the Second World War it was requisitioned as an emergency hospital, following which Harold Wood Hospital was developed within the grounds. The 19th-century house itself remained as the hospital's administrative centre until its closure early in the new millennium.

96 Here, in 1949, the photographer dares to interrupt a meeting in the Matron's office at The Grange where Assistant Matron Flack and Deputy Matron Young report back to Matron Heasman while Miss Chadd, the Matron's secretary, takes the minutes. The stained-glass window and panelled walls are original features, as is the wallpaper—so thick that it had to be fixed to the wall with brass bolts.

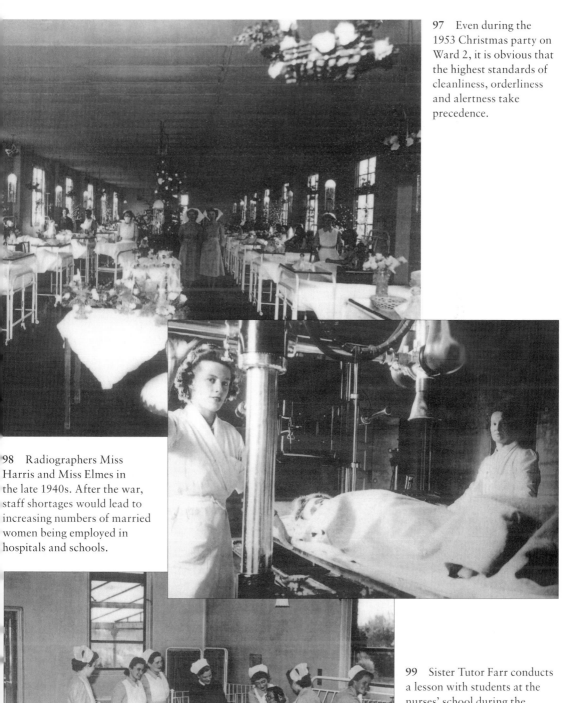

97   Even during the 1953 Christmas party on Ward 2, it is obvious that the highest standards of cleanliness, orderliness and alertness take precedence.

98   Radiographers Miss Harris and Miss Elmes in the late 1940s. After the war, staff shortages would lead to increasing numbers of married women being employed in hospitals and schools.

99   Sister Tutor Farr conducts a lesson with students at the nurses' school during the late 1940s. Perhaps there is something to be learned here by present hospitals from the pristine appearance of the nurses, their white aprons revealing every dirty mark, to the bare ward with nowhere to harbour germs. Incidentally, the nurses' uniform was a very fine green and white stripe.

HAROLD WOOD MINSTRELS Season 1908-9.

CHORUS.

Reading from left to right— BONES—J. Lillystone (Bones) F. Miller (Dusty) E. Wenn (Jimmy) T. Stevens (Willie) Messrs. A. Ladell, C. Saltwell, E. Hitch, O. Hitch,
G. Rainbow, A. Ricketts, W. Muskett, C. Pemberton, Mr. Monks, (Interlocutor) T. Scales, C. Newman, H. Pemberton, J. Cook, G. Harding, F. Harris, A. Ball,
F. Dolberson. TAMBOURINES—H. Wenn (Joey) P. Park (Sam) A. Pearce (Tambo) P. Marshall (Darky) 2nd. Row reading left to right—R. King, F. Putman,
A. Whiting, C. Rae, E. Stokes, F. Marten, D. King, H. Stokes, B. Knightbridge, H. Wenn.

ORCHESTRA.

VIOLINS—Messrs. Woodward, Green, Simmons, Garbe, Wheal, Humphrey CELLO—Mr. Weston. CLARIONET—Mr. Reed. CORNETS—Messrs. Stamp
& Parish. PIANO—A. E. Mazey. Assisted by the following members of the Chorus for the instrumental selections and Part 2 of Programme. VIOLINS—Messrs
Dolberson, Lillystone, H. Pemberton, Rainbow, Saltwell, H. Wenn. 'CELLO—F. J. Park, CORNET—A. Pearce, PIANO—Messrs Muskett & Scales.

100 Although barely conceivable in today's political climate, minstrel entertainment was hugely popular 100 years ago. This impressive assembly of the menfolk of Harold Wood, in what was then called the Entertainment Hall, is indicative of the growth of the village as a community. The hall, in Gubbins Lane, was later dedicated to the memory of those who lost their lives in the First World War and was rechristened 'The Harold Wood Memorial Institute'.

101   In 1926 the Coleman family moved to a new housing development in Gubbins Lane, which according to their daughter, Heather, was then 'a very muddy cart track'. Her father immediately became involved in the social life of the village, instigating the Harold Wood Horticultural Society and organising flower shows like this one in the Memorial Hall *c*.1937. He was also chairman of the local branch of the British Legion for many years.

102   The 'Nippy Nippers' were invited to perform at the British Legion hall following their resounding success at a concert in aid of the War Memorial Institute's extension fund in 1936. The *Romford Times* reported that this youthful band of entertainers, whose ages ranged from about five to 14 years, 'can always be relied upon to supply any audience with an excellent evening's entertainment'.

103   Here, in the latter part of the 1960s, the Memorial Hall is packed mainly with housewives to whom the Women's Institute, formed some forty years earlier, brought wide new interests and outlets for creative activity. Mrs Freeman and her mother are among those in the front row.

104   By the end of the 1930s, Harold Wood's new secondary school was providing its pupils with the opportunity to enjoy such pursuits as sport and drama but, out of school, it was the churches that took most of the responsibility for the social life of the young people in the area. Here, the 1st Harold Wood Ranger Company parades outside the Methodist church, which was then situated in The Drive but has now been relegated to a hall behind the new church building.

105 Affiliated to St Peter, Church of England, the Harold Wood 9th Squirrels Heath Scouts march along Queen's Park Road, where their premises were situated. Note that the boy striding along next to their leader wears clothes of an adult style as was customary after adolescence in the 1950s, before the rock 'n' roll years and the creation of a youth sub-culture.

106 During the war, this would have been a familiar sight as girls in such organisations as the Harold Wood Rangers, seen here in the shed at the Methodist church, immersed themselves in making small, homely items for the use of members of the armed forces. Their captain, Mrs Freeman, is standing at the back.

107 In the summer of 1937, a garden party was held in the grounds of St Chad's, Avenue Road, to help raise funds for the building of St Peter's Church in 1938. The background is dominated by the magnificent poplars lining the road.

108   The house of St Chad's in 1965 before it was converted to Stear's Lodge retirement home.

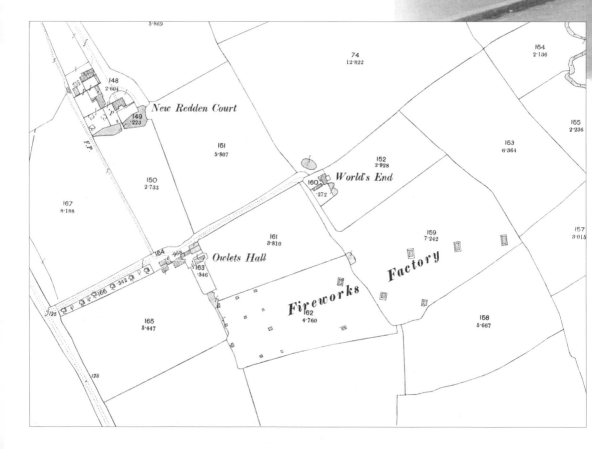

109   The commercial photographer obviously had other pressing commissions as he leapt from his bicycle to take this rather drunken perspective of Avenue Road as it curves away from Station Road. Although many of the original poplars had already been removed, we can catch a glimpse of the former grandeur of what was once the drive to The Grange.

110   (Left) By the end of the 1930s a housing estate occupied the old manorial lands of what had, incongruously, become known as New Redden Court, on the southern side of Squirrels Heath Road. A secondary school would occupy a central position, in the grounds of the demolished ancient manor house. The road running between Owlets Hall and World's End Farm, both also pulled down, would become Coombe Road while the latter building marked the entrance to a park and the new Harold Wood Primary School. The fireworks factory, its buildings spread around to limit any damage caused by an explosion within one of them, was managed by John Brock, son of the owner, who lived in Owlets Hall.

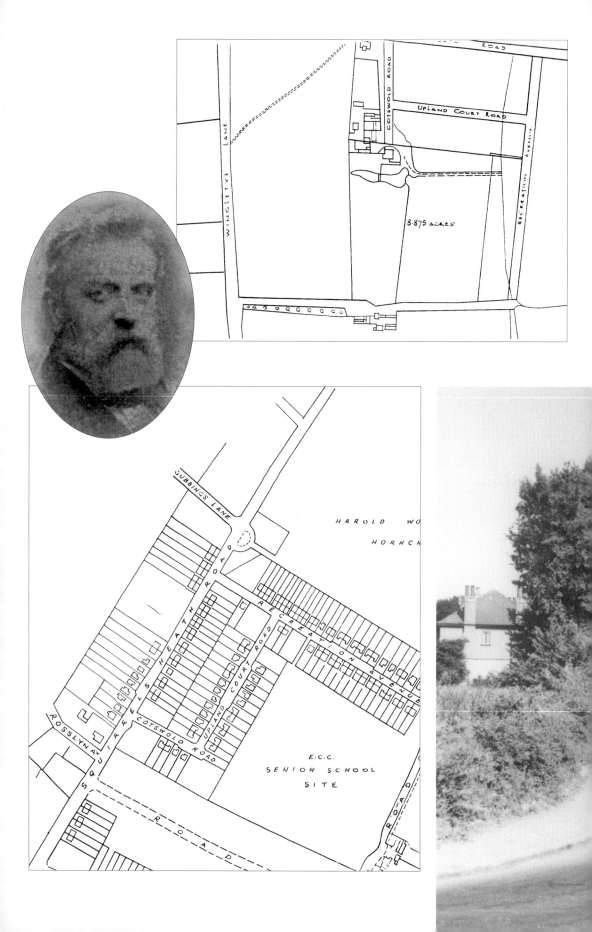

111   (Top left) The first stages in the development of the Redden Court lands in the early 1930s shows the laying out of roads. The name of Upland Court Road depicts its position as a high point in the area while Recreation Avenue denotes its proximity to the new park.

112   (Centre left) The portrait, accompanying an obituary of 1906, might have faded, as could be expected from an early 20th-century newspaper, but it nevertheless captures the integrity that Thomas Rose noted as most characteristic of John Brock. 'Brock' remained an important name in fireworks into the latter part of the 20th century but, after the death of John, the factory was moved to its headquarters at Sutton in Surrey.

113   (Below left) A further stage of development illustrates the position of the New Redden Court Estate in relation to Gubbins Lane.

114   On the boundary of the new estate, shortly after Shepherds Hill merges with Squirrels Heath Road, Gubbins Lane heads towards the railway station. Although this view was captured towards the end of the 1950s, it still possesses a tranquility reminiscent of an earlier period. St Peter's Church, built in 1934 to replace the smaller one in Church Road, stands next to the small school of 1886 which is, today, used as a neighbourhood centre.

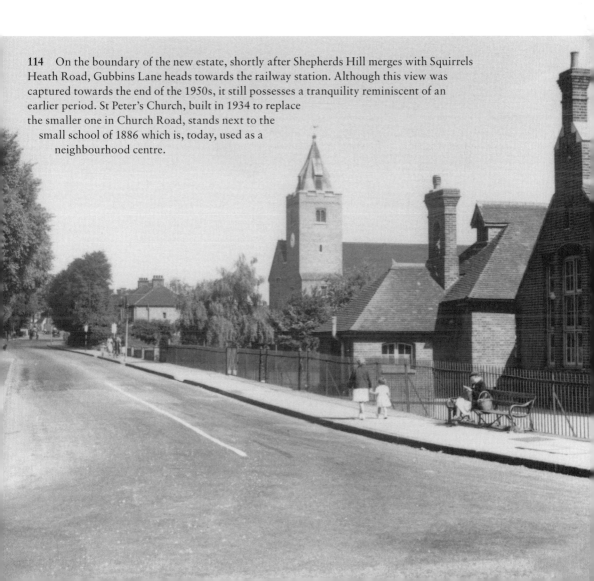

ESSEX
LOCAL EDUCATION AUTHORITY.

NOTICE IS HEREBY GIVEN in accordance with the provisions of Sec. 18 (1) of the Education Act, 1921, that the County Council of Essex, being the Local Education Authority for the purposes of Elementary Education, propose to provide a **NEW PUBLIC ELEMENTARY SCHOOL**, for about 480 Senior Children, in the first instance, on the **NEW REDDEN COURT ESTATE, HAROLD WOOD**, in the **URBAN DISTRICT OF HORNCHURCH.**

The School will be available for the following area :—

HAROLD WOOD and the Adjoining District.

The Managers of any existing School, or any ten ratepayers in the area for which it is proposed to provide the School, may appeal against this proposal by a letter addressed to the Secretary, Board of Education, Whitehall, London, S.W.1, which should reach him within three months from the date of publication of this Notice.

JOHN SARGENT,

Dated 16th April, 1934.   *Director of Education.*

115   The construction of Redden Court Secondary School was long overdue. A senior department, which opened in Ardleigh Green Primary School in 1934, awaited permanent premises that, despite the date in the bottom left-hand corner of this notice, would not open for another four years.

116   The brick-built, two-storey Redden Court School is a typical example of schools constructed by Essex County Council in the 1930s. This view, which appeared in the programme for the official opening of the school, remains very much the same today, overlooking the playing field. However, owing to constrictions of space, the school was destined never to face its main gates and, today, its previous back entrance has been transformed into a modern main entrance.

117 The teachers at the newly opened Redden Court School pose for a formal portrait in 1938 following a four-year sojourn at Ardleigh Green, the more relaxed pose of the centrally seated Mr 'Foxy' Williams befitting his status as headmaster. Three teachers would remain at the school until they reached retirement age: Miss Nunn, standing behind the headmaster; Miss Upton, later Mrs Cook, situated at the far right of the back row; and Mr Higginson, seated in front of her. Mr Wood, seated next to Mr Higginson, was killed in the war.

118 The first Redden Court School prefects pictured in 1938. Jim Smith, the Head Boy, seated in the middle of the second row, was killed in 1940, together with his father and the Eke family, when the garden of his home took a direct hit from a German parachute mine.

119 Shortly after the war, one of the local newspapers photographed an excited group of athletes from 'School' house, which had just wrested the annual sports trophy from the others, 'Squirrel', 'Ardleigh' and 'Hare'.

120 The infamous Leach brothers, Freddy and Charles, who regularly featured in Mr Williams's punishment book, would eventually channel their irrepressible energies into their own business in 1947. The prosperous family-run firm of Harold Wood Coaches operated from its depot in Reginald Road until late in 2000, shortly after which the last of the founder members, Vera, wife of Freddy, died aged eighty-three.

121 In this portrait of Redden Court's Senior XI, the secondary schools' football team finalists for 1951-2, Mr Thomas, on the left, and Mr Herbert were the teachers in charge. In later years the goalkeeper, Sid Purkiss, standing behind the captain, P. Archer, qualified for the 1960 Rome Olympics, competing against the legendary New Zealander Peter Snell in the first heats of the 800 metres.

122 (Above left) These immaculately presented 14-year-old pupils are pictured here in 1959 temporarily separated from the boys in their form. Mr Walsh, the school's third headmaster, ran a tight ship and it is obvious that, although most of these secondary modern school girls may have lacked academic prowess, they could easily equal their counterparts in the grammar school in poise and maturity.

123 (Left) Mr Walsh is pictured here shortly before his retirement in 1965, after 13 years as headmaster. Other long-serving members of staff are Mr Thomas, Mr Broad and Mr Jones (standing first, third and fifth from left), Mr McLaughlin (centre), Mr Higginson and Mr Chisnall (first and third from right), Mrs Avery (sitting second from left), Mrs Wade and Miss Nunn (flanking the headmaster) and Mrs Ascott, the school secretary (far right).

124 (Above) Although the metropolitan Green Belt separating Harold Wood from Brentwood ensured that countryside was close by, it had become common practice in suburban areas to make provision for ornamentally laid-out parks for public recreation. Here, both child and adult would find opportunities for more formally organised leisure time.

125   A young Alf Miller takes his place, on the extreme left of the back row, in the Harold Wood Football Club side for the 1928 Charity Cup final.

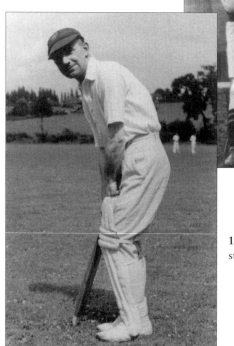

126   In later years, Alf Miller became a stalwart of Harold Wood Cricket Club.

127   The Harold Wood Women's Bowling Club in 1965.

128 From its junction with Gubbins Lane, close to the recreation ground, Squirrels Heath Road gradually merges with Shepherds Hill, which climbs up towards the *Shepherd and Dog* on its way to Upminster Common.

129 Built in 1848 on the once lonely heights of Shepherd's Hill, Harold Wood's other hostelry, the *Shepherd and Dog*, can be viewed here in the early years of the 20th century in its rustic setting. No car park required here; just lean your bicycle up against the picket fence and partake of a pint or two while the chickens outside carry on regardless.

130   Over fifty years later and there are cars aplenty as well as a much larger edifice built in 1929 to accommodate the increase in customers. To the critical eye of the 21st century, it appears to be totally lacking in character but the dominating half-timbered gable, reminiscent of Tudor times, was very much in vogue at the time.

131   At the same time, houses were changing the face of Shepherds Hill, these ones on the Hill Crest Estate, opposite the pub, also mirroring the intra-war fashion for the forward-facing beamed gable. The photographer, Mr Bell of Leigh-on-Sea, deliberately parked his car outside the *Shepherd and Dog* in order to endow the scene with interest and perspective.

Upminster Common

132 At the top of Shepherds Hill lies Upminster Common, which owes its continuing status to the efforts of a local consortium spearheaded by Edward Luther; a struggle for people's rights which went all the way to Parliament. That is why, in this photograph of 1965, and still today, the view across the common towards Harold Hill remains unimpeded by residential development.

133 A century ago there were many rambles that could be taken through roads, lanes and field paths and, in 1911, Romford and Hornchurch were commended for erecting copious 'finger posts' to mark the way. Here, in 1920, the common stretches beyond the crossroads at the junction of Nag's Head Lane, Hall Lane, Shepherds Hill in Harold Wood and Warley Hill in Brentwood.

134 Astonishingly, some ten years later, when the motorcar was in the process of usurping the old order, a permanent first-aid station, with ambulance on stand-by, was set up at an accident black spot where the rural Hall Lane and Bird Lane had been bisected by the A127 Southend Arterial Road, on the southernmost margin of the hamlet of Upminster Common.

135 The job seems hardly onerous here but volunteers from the Upminster and Hornchurch St John Ambulance have arrived in preparation for the equivalent of the rush hour of the time. The dangerous potential of the unfamiliar, fast motorcars had been recognised when they claimed their first victim, Ben Gray, 81 years old, who was knocked down and killed in 1931 while crossing the A127 to visit the shop in Bird Lane.

136 The shop Ben was making his way to from his home in Hall Lane was situated in that part of Bird Lane stranded by the arterial road. Owned by one of his relatives, Maude Clutton, it would remain open until 1936 in one of the late 19th-century pantile cottages, photographed here in the mid-1950s by Mr Fitzwilliams, a postcard publisher from Seven Kings who had scented profit in the area.

137 In 1843 the sparse housing of the Upminster Common community spilled down Hall Lane and Bird Lane, which came together at the far boundary of the hamlet at the pottery works. In 1925 the A127 would drive through both roads just above this junction. In the lower part of the map can be seen the houses of Lilliput and Lambkins, which were to feature in the poetry of Edward Thomas.

138 Following the construction of the arterial road, the major part of Bird Lane, to the north of the A127, would be renamed Tomkins Lane after the magnificent 15th-century hall house of Great Tomkyns, one of Havering's few remaining old buildings.

139 During the 19th century, the rural atmosphere of Bird Lane was disturbed by the busy industry of the brick and pottery works at its lower end. Together with the sewage works in Hall Lane, this was the main source of income for the common's small population.

140 (Left) This solemnly staged photograph of labourers at the Upminster Brick Kilns early in the 20th century emphasises the stillness needed for the long exposure time required by the early camera: all, including the horse, appear to be holding their breath.

141 At 6.30 a.m. on 7 August 1944, the sleepy hamlet of Upminster Common was rudely awoken by a V1 'doodlebug' rocket making landfall in Hall Lane. The chapel and three adjacent cottages were reduced to rubble.

142   The one fatality was Mary Holman, aged 75, who lived in Tyes Cottage close to the chapel, seen here at the top of the photograph. She died of her wounds two days later in Harold Wood Emergency Hospital and is commemorated 'in perpetuity' by the Commonwealth Graves Commission.

143   In the year 1850, a small band of country folk unanimously decided to give of their time and resources to erect a chapel: the Upminster Common Mission.

144   In 1947 another chapel rose from the ashes in the form of two army huts, thanks to generous donations. Three years later, a centenary service was held there to commemorate the opening of the first chapel, 'a wayside sanctuary, standing in one of the quietest and most rural parts of the Essex countryside'.

Harold Park and Sunnytown

145 In contrast to the heights of Upminster Common, Harold Park lies in a valley on the north-eastern fringe of Harold Wood. The fine Victorian house 'Woodlawn' was once the last house in the village before Paines Brook, which marks the boundary between Harold Wood and its suburb.

146 The shadowy form of the photographer is also immortalised as he captures this inviting group in the 1930s with his Brownie box camera, the new technology enabling him to take a 'snap' shot of their easy intimacy. The proprietor of the dairy in Church Road, Harry Guy, poses nonchalantly with a milk churn against one of the cart shafts. On his death, he bequeathed enough money for the people of Harold Park to buy a field for recreational purposes.

147 (Above) This aerial view shows the expansion taking place in the grounds of Harold Court Mansion when it became a T.B. sanatorium and wooden wards, open to all weathers, were erected around the central lawned area. Built by a founder member of the ill-fated consortium intending to develop Harold Wood as a township, it had earlier become a lunatic asylum and later a teachers' training college before its final incarnation as residential flats.

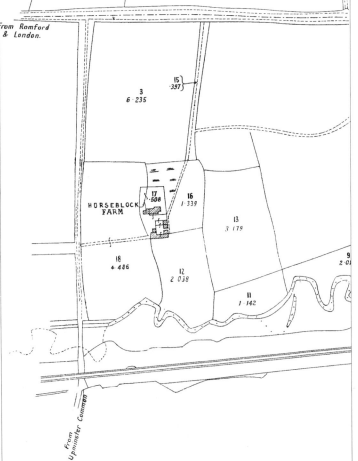

148 (Left) Sandwiched between the Colchester Road and the railway line, the land of Horseblock Farm, seen here in 1895, would eventually be occupied by Sunnytown's rows of identical bungalows, the track on the left becoming Harold Court Road and the drive leading to the farmhouse initially envisaged as The Greenway.

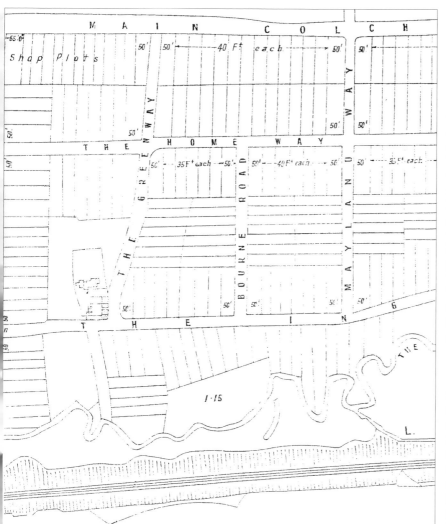

The plan shows a map with labels including:

MAIN COLCH

Shop Plots

THE GREENWAY

THE HOMEWAY

BOURNE ROAD

MAYLAND

WAY

THE INGREWAY

THE ... L.

1·15

50' markings (50', 40 Ft each, 35 Ft each, etc.)

149 (Left) Some thirty years later, it is the meandering river which is confined between the geometry of the roads and the railway. The layout of the roads in this plan of 1924 would change somewhat before building began: the vertically placed roads of The Greenway and Bourne Road would disappear entirely, with The Greenway being reinstated on a parallel line between The Homeway and The Ingreway, all three of which would, in time, drop the definite article.

150 (Below) The motorcar was such a remote sight in the 1920s that Sunnytown roads were constructed as 'ways' with no need for road or pavement, as this early photograph of The Greenway will testify.

151 (Below) Only a decade later and the area is firmly established as part of Harold Park, the epithet of Sunnytown consigned to the past. This postcard of Greenway mirrors exactly the development of its sister roads, Homeway and Ingreway, in anticipation of an increase in motor traffic.

152 (Right) The newly numbered A12 is certainly 'geared up' for the age of the motorcar in the early 1930s as the old Roman road sweeps through Harold Park on its way to Colchester, as it had done since time immemorial when the town was a Roman stronghold.

153 Close by in Harold Park, at a similar time, the presence of the car in the background reminds us that, although the transition to mechanisation on the farm would be a slow one, it was certainly inevitable.

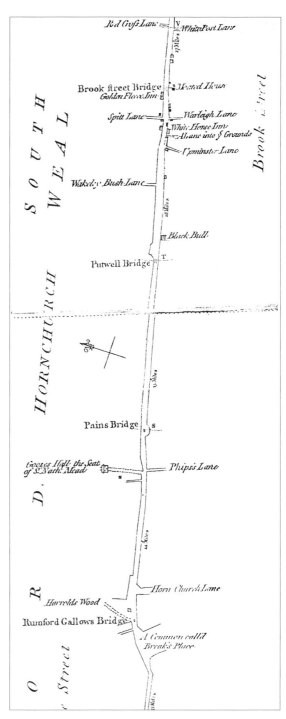

154 An extract from the Middlesex and Essex Turnpike Trust map of 1768 shows the Great Essex Road, formerly a Roman road and today the A12, where it rises from what is now Gallow's Corner. Phips's Lane, which will be renamed Gubbins Lane, points towards the site of present-day Harold Wood and, directly opposite, the drive to Goozes Hall will become Gooshayes Drive, leading into the centre of modern Harold Hill.

155   Close to the boundary separating the parishes of Hornchurch and South Weald, at Brook Street, stood this 18th-century octagonal toll booth; yet another example of a small piece of vernacular history being ruthlessly swept away in the name of progress, in this case to make way for the widening of what would become the A12 London to Colchester Road.

156   The Parade was specifically built to serve the residents of Harold Park but, facing onto the Colchester Road as it did, a number of cafés opened up to attract a growing number of passing motorists. The postcard can reliably be placed in 1934 from the Mayfair cinema poster advertising the Academy Award-winning film *One Night of Love* starring Grace Moore.

157   The other side of the road was the scene of a wartime tragedy, witnessed by 10-year-old Geoff Walton, when a young pilot, attempting to nurse his crippled Hurricane to the nearby emergency landing ground at the old aerodrome of Maylands, crashed into a house close to the junction of the main road with Woodstock Avenue, directly opposite The Parade. Nobody was injured and, today, a plaque on the side of the house commemorates the bravery of Pilot Officer Pattullo.

158   Pilot Officer William 'Billy' Blair Pattullo was born in Chile of Scottish parentage. Having seen so many of his comrades in 46 Squadron lose their lives in the Battle of Britain, he was stoical about his own chances of survival, saying, 'You never know when your ticket's going to come up,' and in response when his sister urged him to take care, 'I'll do my best, but we've got to finish the job.' He was killed in action on 25 October 1940 at Harold Park.

159   Billy's father kept the treasured photograph in a leather wallet, listing on the back of the picture what later proved to be an incomplete record of his son's achievements or 'kills'. One of the most successful pilots in his squadron, he was due to receive the Distinguished Flying Cross, which, sadly, cannot be awarded posthumously.

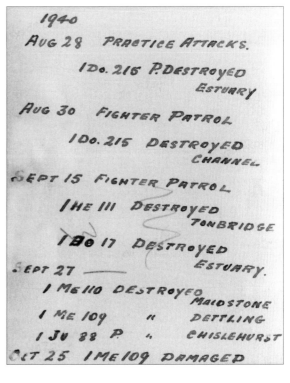

160 Although unofficial photography was prohibited, someone managed to capture a glimpse of the aftermath of Harold Wood's worst wartime incident when a V2 rocket landed in David Drive on 13 February 1945, claiming 14 lives.

161 At the neighbouring Harold Court School, the impersonal headmaster's log recorded none of the human devastation, just damage to the fabric of the school and its consequent role as first-aid post and headquarters for the Civil Defence services.

1945.

Jan. 9 Miss Gallaway returned from Norfolk.
P. Roe of the L.L.S. started a teaching trial

12 On roll. 258. Av. Att.:- 209.8.

19. On roll: 260. Av. Att.:- 207.5.

26 On roll: 260. Av. Att.:- 197.3.

30. A heavy fall of snow caused the attendance to drop to 139/263 (53.0%).

Feb. 2 The school speech-therapist called today re Maureen Scanlan
P. Roe finished his teaching trial
On roll:- 263. Av. att.:- 185.6.

9. Mrs. Bartlett called today
On roll:- 258. Av. Att.:- 228.8

13. At 6.46 p.m. this evening, a rocket fell near the school & caused extensive damage to tiles, glass, doors, etc. The building was used as a F.A.P., and H.Q. for the C.D. services, I being in charge.

14 School closed. Mrs. Brown absent, injured last night

15. The canteen opened today & milk was served. Some 40 children came.
Miss Heppel's class resumed work.
On roll: 258.

162   The Harold Court football team features Courtney Kitching, seated in the middle of the front row, who would become the first president of the Redden Court Past Pupils' Association. War is not far away and John Grace, seated on the ground, would be another young witness to the Hurricane crashing in 1940 as he shopped at The Parade. He recalled the arrival of one of the huge R.A.F. lorries, nicknamed 'Queen Marys', to take away the wreckage of the plane almost at the same time as the ambulance which came to take the injured pilot to hospital.

163   Courtney appears, once more, as captain of the cricket team. Two years later, when attending the local secondary school, he was encouraged to keep a diary, in which the mundane sat, unaffectedly, side by side with the momentous. An extract from 5 September 1941 is fairly typical: 'The Russians are still holding the Germans back on the outskirts of Leningrad. I went out to play on my barrow in the evening.'

164 The 14-year-old Len Rogers, current chairman of the Redden Court P.P.A., was the only one able to record for posterity the Geoffrey Avenue street party held to celebrate V.E. Day in 1945. Several people owned cameras by then but it was virtually impossible to buy any film.

Ardleigh Green

165 Mr Bell, the photographer, has once again purposely left his car in the picture to add interest to the scene. He has come all the way from Leigh-on-Sea to photograph a new series of picture postcards in the ever-expanding area of Harold Wood and Ardleigh Green *c*.1930. By now, the Southend Arterial Road has already swept through Ardleigh Green and Wingletye Lane, severing the ancient community's links with the old lands of Redden Court. Here, on the Harold Wood side of the new main road, the stranded lower part of Wingletye Lane has been renamed Redden Court Road.

166 On 25 March 1925, all the children in Hornchurch and Romford were given a day off school to be present at the official opening of the arterial road, London to Southend, by HRH Prince Henry, son of George V and uncle to our present queen. In total four arches were built at intervals along the road for separate opening ceremonies at Woodford, Ardleigh Green, Rayleigh and Southend.

167 The road was not the busy dual carriageway that we know today but, as part of the revolutionary network of transport arteries running from the heart of the city to its various outposts, it was deemed deserving of the royal stamp of approval. The presence of Prince Henry was particularly appropriate as he had embraced the new technology with more enthusiasm than many of the horse-loving royal fraternity.

168 The brand new road crosses Harold Wood railway bridge just at the point where the track leaves Ardleigh Green to enter the cutting leading towards Harold Wood Station. The splendid tarmac surface is a tribute to J.L. Macadam, who devised this smooth, dust-free crust, first applied as a road surface in 1907 after motorcars with pneumatic tyres had been admitted to the public roads in 1896.

169 It is 1958 and the postcard is still being used in preference to the telephone to let a friend know that one had arrived home safely. In its small way, it helps to chart the development of the area looking along the Squirrels Heath Road from Ardleigh Green towards Harold Wood, both separated by the arterial road running across the picture.

170 Twenty years before, in order to profit from the increased traffic on the arterial road, the small Bridge Garage had opened opposite the piece of waste ground so carefully cultivated in the previous photograph, on the corner of the arterial road and Ardleigh Green Road.

171 Returning to the more
congested years of the late 1950s and
early 1960s, a Hillman Minx crosses
the arterial road from Harold Wood
into what had originally been part
of Squirrels Heath Road but was
later redesignated as Ardleigh Green
Road. Perhaps the car will turn right
into the expanded premises of Bridge
Garage.

172 The roof and clock are
the only recognisable features
of the earlier business, which
has begun to specialise in
streamlined, sporty model
cars.

173 Fifty years earlier, Ardleigh Green Road was a simple
country lane bordered by ditches. Of the distinctive conifers,
which lined the road on the right for a considerable
distance, only a few survive among today's densely
packed houses opposite Nelmes Way. To the left of the
road is the northern boundary of Little Nelmes
Farm and the parkland of the ancient house
of Great Nelmes, which, by 1909,
was being developed on garden
suburb lines similar to
neighbouring Emerson
Park, built on the
southern edge of
the estate.

174 A group of residents is photographed outside the local sweetshop, whose name reflects the striking line of trees opposite, in the type of frozen pose essential if they were not to blur the image while the glass plate slowly developed. The formal tableau mirrors a small piece of social history indicating the importance placed on hats in Edwardian times. The shop survives today as a sandwich bar at No. 88, Ardleigh Green Road, one of a terrace of three cottages built in the first half of the 19th century.

175 The Ardleigh Green Baptist Church, which had been erected in 1914, is pictured here in the 1920s: a tiny corrugated iron building just visible by the side of the tree in the extreme left of the photograph. The present brick building was erected in 1932 on land given to the church by Richard Banyard of Little Nelmes Farm, Ernest Pearson, jeweller of Romford, and Thomas England, chemist of Romford.

176 In the early 1950s, looking in the direction of Hornchurch, fir trees are still part of the scenery. On the left, Carter's bakery, here also housing a post office, had been owned by the same family since the late 1800s, occupying the premises of an even older bakehouse.

177 The coat of arms of the once distinguished family of Banyard, by 1918 the local dairy farmer, was adopted by Ardleigh Green Primary School in 1950.

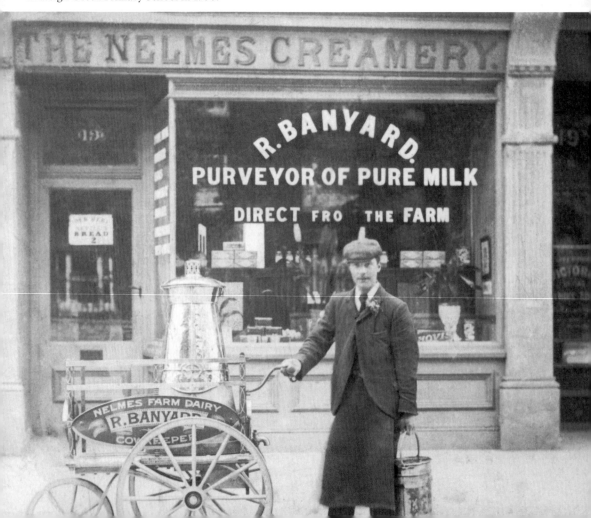

178 Although this postcard was labelled Ardleigh Green Road, there is a suspicion that it might, in fact, be Squirrels Heath Lane, which is a turning off it. Whatever its true identity, it is clear that, shortly before the Second World War, the area was losing its rural appeal as trees in both roads were being torn up in preparation for house building.

179 As Ardleigh Green expanded after the war, Cecil Avenue was representative of the type of development taking place beyond both sides of the main road.

180 (Above left) A.R.P. report centres charted all enemy action directed at civilians during the Second World War, recording, via telephone, the stages of each critical moment. This page from a telephone message pad, dated 15 November 1940, relayed details of the incident in Cecil Avenue in which the Eke and Smith families lost their lives.

181 (Above centre) A casualty of another sort was the vernacular heritage of the hamlet, which fell victim to greedy developers who would show no mercy to these small cottages, their ancient timbered framework protected by weatherboarding. They stood on the corner of Cecil Avenue until replaced by shops.

182 (Right) The distinction between Ardleigh Green, where these two avenues were actually situated, and neighbouring Gidea Park was deliberately blurred in an effort to profit from the post-war development of the more prestigious Gidea Park garden suburb.

183 (Right) Stafford Avenue was a scene of devastation in 1945 when a V2 rocket landed on the Lacrinoid plastics factory, killing three.

184 Some of the youngsters in Birch Crescent, who had not been evacuated, amuse themselves during wartime. They are, from front to back: Ray Hare, Cyril Birch, Alan Bridges, Terry Wilson, Neil O'Donnelly and Ron Kelly.

185 (Left) Although a horse-drawn cart was not an uncommon sight right up until the beginning of the 1960s, someone in Birch Crescent was quick to recognise a photographic opportunity when it presented itself. The firm of Fella Brothers was the supremo of the local ice-cream sellers, running an ice-cream parlour in Billet Lane, Hornchurch.

186 (Bottom left) Sandwiched between detached houses of the 1930s, these small 19th-century cottages on Ardleigh Green Road were demolished in the latter part of the 1950s to make way for the rebuilding of the church of All Saints, Squirrels Heath, which had been destroyed in the war. Intense public indignation was aroused at the relocation of a Romford church to the parish of Hornchurch in order to provide for the growing population in the vicinity of the Southend Arterial Road. There was a feeling that the diocesan authorities had succeeded where Hitler had failed, in breaking the spirit of the congregation.

187 (Below) Today the rancour accompanying the move has long since abated, remembered only by older members of the original church but, although the parish boundaries were redrawn to enable the church to remain in the ecclesiastical parish of Squirrels Heath, Gidea Park, most of the present parishioners regard it as belonging to Ardleigh Green.

188 The rambling Victorian Ardleigh House, part of the Great Nelmes Estate, managed to escape demolition when purchased in 1946 by Essex County Council, together with 11 acres of land, for 'Service of Youth, Community Centre and playing fields'. It has survived into the 21st century to fulfil a similar role in the neighbourhood.

189 Ardleigh House Youth Football Club, 1954-6.

190   Many more shops were springing up to cater for the rising population at the beginning of the 1930s, including two shopping parades, photographed here at the beginning of the 1960s. The original Smy's drapery, on the corner of Squirrels Heath Lane and Ardleigh Green Road, has been renamed 'Westwear' while a private house, its ground floor also used as shop premises, has been built on a drive which originally separated the two shopping parades. The primary school can just be distinguished on the far right.

191   As the camera focuses on the second shopping parade, close to the school, it has become increasingly obvious how valuable cars have proved in aiding the dating of photographs. Here, the van close to Carter's bakery and the *Spencer's Arms* might be distinctly of the 1920s but the rest of the traffic places the scene firmly in the 1930s and, of course, the school opened in 1933.

192 (Above) It might not seem an obvious subject for a multi-view postcard but the opening of council schools, from the late 1920s, was a milestone in the history of universal education. Each photograph is linked to the motto of the Ardleigh Green Mixed Junior and Infants' School, which seems rather dated nowadays: 'Work hard and Play the Game'.

193 (Above right) The actors in the junior school play 'Fairyland' are photographed in 1936 in a variety of party dresses and home-made costumes. Pyjamas were worn by the 'pillow fight' elves, of which one was Vera Harrison, lounging to the left of the front row, now secretary of the Redden Court P.P.A.

194 (Right) Throughout its history, Ardleigh Green School has earned a well-deserved reputation for its country dancing. In 1958, two groups perform in front of temporary classrooms built in 1934 to accommodate senior pupils awaiting the construction of Redden Court Secondary School. The enormous tree to the left of the photograph was then a mere sapling. It has survived into the 21st century.

195 Mr Pryce-Rees, the headmaster, standing on the right, and Mr Luckock, his deputy, share the pride of the 1957-8 winners of the district cup who beat Ayloff Primary School on goal average.

196 The programme marks the unveiling of the school crest in 1950. It is an adaptation of the arms and crest of the local Banyard family, which can trace its ancestry back to 1066 when the arms were first carried at the Battle of Hastings by two brothers who hailed from Normandy. The crest did not appear until the reign of Henry VIII. The heraldic description of a lion's paw surmounting the shield is incorrect. It has been found to be a bear's paw with a ragged edge, as if torn from the body, decorated with a golden bird. The other birds are Cornish choughs. The motto, which replaced the earlier school one of 'Work hard and play the game', comes from an old Welsh school motto.

Index

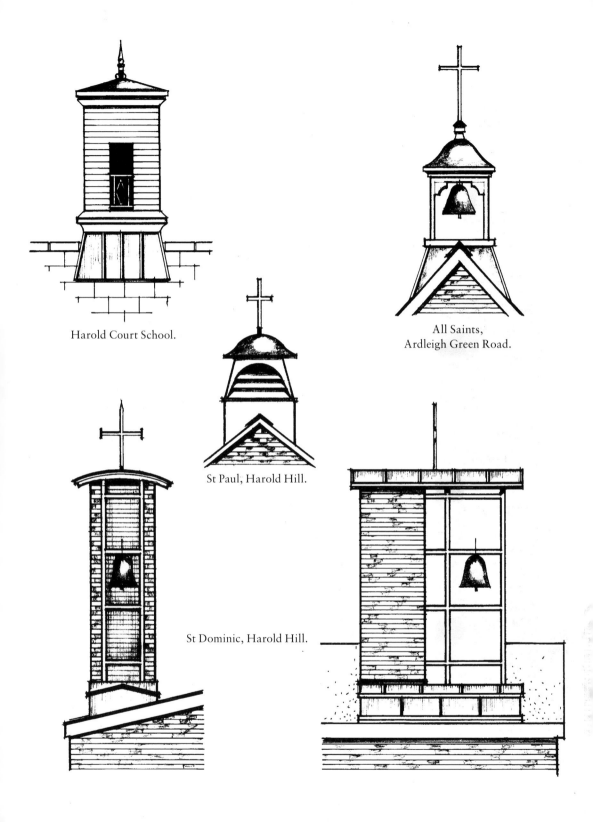

Harold Court School.

All Saints,
Ardleigh Green Road.

St Paul, Harold Hill.

St Dominic, Harold Hill.